Romans

The Road to Righteousness

A Bible Study Guide
by Charles Brock

Published by Church Growth International, Inc.
13174 Owens Lane
Neosho, MO

All Scripture quotations are from *Today's English Version*
unless otherwise stated.

ISBN: 1-885504-26-8

Contents

Suggested Use

Romans: The Road to Righteousness has been prepared to assist believers in better understanding Paul's Letter to the Romans. The Bible is the textbook. This study guide is to be used as a resource and help in the study of the Scripture. Read the Scripture first, then read the chapter from this book.

Prayer and humility are essentials for the teacher and students. Some parts will not be fully understood. This calls for humility. Other parts will be understood if you prayerfully depend upon God's enlightenment.

Introduction to the
Letter to the Romans

The letter could be called the Gospel to the Romans because all the essentials of the Gospel are found in it. It is the first great work of Christian theology and perhaps the greatest ever written.

There seems to be no question that Paul wrote this letter. He claims to be the writer. (Romans 1:1,7) The style, vocabulary, teachings, and doctrines are consistent with the other writings of Paul.

The letter was written after Paul had completed his missionary work in the eastern provinces and was preparing to go to Jerusalem. (15:19-25) He was going to deliver the love offering which was raised in the new churches in Greece and Asia Minor for the poor people in the Jerusalem church. (15:26-28) This trip was probably the one described in Acts 20. Paul was in Greece when he wrote the letter to the Romans. (Acts 20:2-3) It is generally believed he was in the city of Corinth.

The probable date of writing was A.D. 57 or 58.

The letter was sent to the church in Rome. We do not know when the church in Rome was started, but a close study of history indicates Christianity seemed to have been introduced in Rome before A.D. 49.

It is not known who founded the church in Rome. Paul's letter reveals he had never been to Rome. Some may suggest Peter as the founder, but Peter was still in Jerusalem when Paul visited there about A.D. 48 or 49. A little later Peter was in Antioch. This means the church in Rome was already in existence while Peter was still in Jerusalem and Antioch.

Paul had more than one purpose for writing the letter. It is clear he planned to go to Spain and would pass through Rome. He was asking the church in Rome to help him make the trip. (15:23-24) Paul also had a strong desire to fellowship with the Roman believers. (1:8-14) From these factors we conclude that Paul wrote to prepare the Roman Christians for his visit to Rome, but he had a greater purpose in writing. He proposed to give a complete view of his position of how God makes a person righteous.

In this study, we will pursue the theme, "How God makes a person righteous." (1:16-17)

The letter has two clear divisions:
    Doctrinal, chapters 1-11
    Practical, chapters 12-16

The letter must be approached with prayer and humility. Though it may be difficult to comprehend the full meaning of every part, the message is for today.

ROMANS 1

Introduction of the Writer and His Message

Outline

1. Salutation 1:1-7

   a. Paul Introduces Himself 1:1
   b. Identifies His Message 1:2-4
   c. Gives His Credentials 1:5-6

2. Personal Greeting 1:8-15

   a. Prayer of Thanksgiving 1:8-10
   b. Paul's Missionary Spirit 1:11-15

3. Theme of the Letter 1:16-17

4. Man's Problem: Sin 1:18-32

Salutation 1:1-7

Only a person secure in who he is would introduce himself as a servant. Paul was not expressing a false humility. He literally thought of himself as a slave to Jesus Christ and a servant to humanity. He knew he was chosen and called by God and he knew the work God gave him was to preach the Good News.

After a short introduction of himself, Paul identifies his message, the Good News God called him to preach. He reminds the Romans that the Good News was promised by God in the Scriptures. The Good News is that God's Son, Jesus Christ, came in the flesh into the world. In His humanity, He was a descendant of David who had been a beloved king in Jewish history. He was shown to be the divine Son of God by being raised from death.

Paul then gives his own credentials. He says through Jesus, God called him to be an apostle in order to bring people to God. These people included the Christians in Rome to whom he was writing. His authority was his call from God. He understood that his God-given responsibility was also a privilege.

When a person knows God has called him to do something, it is easier to remain faithful in that work. Every pastor and teacher should be aware of a clear call from God.

In verse 7 Paul is saying it is because of the call and the work given to him by God that he is writing to the Christians in Rome. He reminds them that God loves them and has called them also. He prays for grace and peace for them.

Paul uses the word "grace" 88 times in his writings. He always put grace before peace, knowing peace can come only after grace has been experienced.

Personal Greetings 1:8-15

Paul assured the Christians in Rome of his genuine love and concern for them which caused him to pray often for them. He wanted to visit them, not only to be a blessing to them and help strengthen their faith, but so they might also be a blessing to him.

All believers need to remember that they never become so strong in their faith that they do not need the help of fellow believers.

Paul's missionary spirit is seen in verses 11-15. With his call and obligation came an eagerness to carry out the work God had given him. He had a burning desire to preach the Good News to all people no matter what their circumstances were. Although he felt a deep obligation to preach to Gentiles, he was also eager to bring the message to Jews.

Preachers today should have this same feeling of urgency, even before they have received special training. The sense of urgency comes with the call, not with the training.

Theme of the Letter 1:16-17

When the Gospel is preached, something always happens in the heart of the preacher and in the hearts of the hearers. It is God's power that produces conviction and salvation. 1:16

Verses 16 and 17 give the theme of Paul's letter to the Romans: **How God makes a person righteous.**

The word "righteous" can be simply defined as right standing with God. God puts people in right standing with Himself through their faith in Him. Paul says it is faith from beginning to end. Not only are we saved by faith, we must also live by faith.

Man's Problem: Sin 1:18-32

Paul now begins to lay some background for the teaching of how God makes a person righteous. He paints a graphic picture of a person in sin. This is the logical place to begin because the road to righteousness begins with the recognition of sin. Sin is what keeps people from right standing with God.

As we begin a study of the sinful nature and its consequences, let us note some characteristics of sin.

1. Sin has no nature of its own; it is a parasite.
2. Sin is self-centered.
3. Sin is destructive.
4. Sin's presence gives no immediate pain, causing a person to believe nothing is wrong.
5. Sin's power lies in the force of delusion.
6. Sin desensitizes as it grows.
7. Sin produces a false self.
8. Sin will cause a person to become blind to evil.

Cancer in its early stages brings no pain or discomfort. It starts on the inside and destroys unless it is discovered for the person. That is the way sin works.

Some results of sin

1. Sin causes a person to take the worth and dignity from being founded in God and put self on the throne.

Human nature is centered in self, making self to be god. Sin brings self-deceit. The first stage of honesty is self-honesty.

2. Sin causes a person to be intolerant of anything that overshadows himself.

One of the greatest indoor sports of people in modern society is to tear down anything or anybody that appears to be bigger than themselves. Pride causes a person to want to stay ahead of everyone else. To do this, he often criticizes others in an effort to bring them down below himself. This is murder, character assassination. People in general have the same characteristics as the crucifiers of Christ and today would crucify Him again.

3. Sin causes people to experience progressive deterioration of character. Life becomes perverted—self-centered rather than others-centered.

4. Sin causes people to be utterly alone. There is inward warfare, inward division. People begin to depend on themselves and leave no room for God. Without God they do not have what it takes to live a full and meaningful life.

We need to understand the difference between sin and sins.

- ◆ Sin is the root; sins are the fruit.
- ◆ Sin is the disease; sins are the symptoms.
- ◆ Sin is unbelief; sins are the marks of unbelief.

Now let us look more closely at verses 18-32.

Sin causes people to suppress the truth about God. 1:18-23

God has made Himself known to mankind from the beginning. His eternal power and divine nature are seen in His creation but people have refused to see. Their denial of God seems to make them blind to God's anger against sin and evil.

With the refusal to see God as He is, people's thoughts become confused. Their minds are filled with darkness. Instead of worshipping God, they come to the unreasonable point of worshipping man-made images or creations of God. People of today have added many other objects of worship. Wealth, pleasure, fame, beauty—these are things many people worship.

Sin causes a person to cast off all restraint. 1:24-32

These verses give a horrible picture of sin. People without God pervert the natural things of life. Homosexuality is depicted here as the ultimate perversion in human relationships.

At the first reading of these verses we seem to see only the sins of sensuality. Look again at verses 28-31. We see that jealousy, deceit, gossip, speaking evil of others, disobedience to parents, boastfulness, and failure to keep promises are also fruits of a perverted nature.

Paul succeeds in making it clear that all are sinners, beginning with the Gentiles. In the next chapter he will show that while the Gentiles without the Law are sinners, the Jews with the Law are also sinners.

Application and Participation

1. What characteristics of a great person are seen in Paul?
   Slave to Christ Servant of Humanity

2. How can a person know that he is called to be a preacher or pastor? Witness of God's Spirit

3. Name at least two main parts of the Gospel found in verses 3 and 4. *Humanity & Divinity of Jesus*

4. What is the theme of the letter to the Romans? In which verses is the theme found? *Righteous v16-17*

5. Righteousness means *right standing before God.*

6. What is sin? — *A parasite*

7. What is the difference between sin and sins? *Sin is the disease. Sins are the symptoms*

8. How is sin like cancer? *Destroys a person from the inside out*

9. Name some sins often seen in the lives of respectable church members. *Jealousy, envy, slander, gossip, Pride, deceitful, Immorality.*

10. As sinners saved by grace, the only thing we have to boast about is the grace of God. True *✓* False ___

Verses to memorize: Romans 1:14,15,16

ROMANS 2

The Guilt of All Mankind

Outline

1. God's Judgment 2:1-16

2. The Jews and the Law 2:17-29

In the latter part of chapter 1, Paul spoke of the guilt of the Gentiles—all people who were not Jews. The Jews considered the Gentiles to be pagans. Without a doubt, the Jews were in full agreement as they read of the guilt of the Gentiles.

Paul now turns to **the position of the Jews before a righteous God**. Jews believed that because they had the Law, they were in right standing with God. Paul tells them they, too, are sinners. Gentiles are sinners without the Law; Jews are sinners with the Law. Paul is moving toward the conclusion in Romans 3:23 that all people, whether Jew or Gentile, are under the judgment of God.

Paul had made strong accusations about man's guilt before God. He painted a vivid, unpleasant picture of man's sinful condition. It is true that he was speaking of the Gentiles in chapter 1. But he knew that the Jews were sinners also, and he knew how they responded when confronted with the subject of sin.

The Jews sought to escape the accusation, "You are a sinner," in two different ways.

One group tried to escape the accusation by assuming the spectator's viewpoint. 2:1-16

A spectator is one who views others, passes judgment on their lives and actions, and ignores self. (2:1-3) These people acknowledged the truth but would not relate themselves to it.

One of the most damaging parts of sin is its power to blind a person to the fact that he is a sinner. The Jews were self-righteous. They enjoyed pointing to "bad sinners."

Spectators are often the biggest hypocrites. They sit in judgment over others in matters where they, also, are guilty. When a person bows his head in sorrow, sheds a tear, and says honestly, "I am a sinner," there is progress.

In these verses Paul is emphasizing that God judges all people with one set of standards. The self-righteous and the sensual will sit in the same judgment. Every person is involved in life and will be judged according to his deeds.

Another group tried to avoid the accusation, "You are a sinner," by being religious. 2:17-29

The Jews relied on the Law. They boasted of being religious, considering themselves God's favorites. They thought they had special privileges because God had chosen them and blessed them as a nation. They found it difficult to think of themselves as sinners. They felt they were leaders of the blind (sinners) and knew everything because they had been taught the Law.

This is a trap a "good Christian" can easily fall into. There is one thing absent when a person is shielding self with religion: that is a feeling that he is a sinner. This kind of person is often involved in religious activity—so involved that he has little time to see himself as a sinner. Spiritual and moral pride appear. This religious person can actually become proud of being humble.

One of the greatest blessings is to know self to be a sinner. Only from this stance can a person know God.

The Jews tried to escape the accusation of being sinners by hiding behind the Law. Paul said Gentiles were sinners without the Law; Jews were sinners under the Law. The conclusion: All are sinners.

Who is the real Jew? 2:25-29

We might ask who is the real Christian. Paul is asking what really matters to God; is it the person who claims the title or is it the one who is actually trying to follow Christ?

What really matters? What is genuine? It is a real love for that which God has done in Christ Jesus. This love is spontaneous, natural, and does not call for man's praise or approval. 2:29

Application and Participation

1. What is the major subject matter in chapter 2?

2. Why do people not want to admit to being sinners?

3. What is the relationship of privilege and responsibility?

4. What was the responsibility of the Jew?

5. What is our responsibility today?

6. If a church leader admits he has a struggle with sin, will he lose people's respect?

7. Was Paul making a mistake when he confessed to being the worst of sinners? 1 Timothy 1:15

8. What are the two responses given to the accusation, "You are a sinner?"

9. Is it possible for us to become spectators and point to other sinners and forget we are sinners saved by grace?

10. How will it help Mr. Outsider (unsaved) if Christians stop being so self-righteous?

ROMANS 3

Man's Predicament and God's Plan

Outline

1. Jews, Gentiles, and a Faithful God 3:1-8

2. Man's Predicament 3:9-18

3. God's Plan 3:19-31

    a. Man is not made right with God by keeping the Law. 3:20
    b. God's plan is made clear. 3:21-31

Jews, Gentiles, and a Faithful God 3:1-8

In chapter 2 Paul pointed out to the Jews that even though they had the Law, they were sinners, just like the Gentiles without the Law. He begins chapter 3 with some final remarks about the Jews and their relationship to God. If Jews are sinners just as the Gentiles are, do Jews have any advantage over Gentiles? Paul says, "Yes, indeed!" God had entrusted His message to the Jews first. (3:2) This increases their accountability to God. To those who receive much, much is expected.

God pledged to bless the Jews, but this blessing was related to the fulfillment of a task. The Jews majored on the privilege of being God's chosen people and forgot the task He gave them.

They thought they were God's favorites. This is an attitude not pleasant to be around.

Even though the Jews be unfaithful (3:3), God will be faithful in His promises and judgment. (3:4) This shows there is no favoritism with God. He will be faithful to punish sin where He sees it, with both Jew and Gentile. Paul thought God was right in condemning the Jews because of their unfaithfulness.

Some Jews were faithful and were called the faithful remnant. The unfaithful lost their privileges and were under judgment.

In chapters 9-11 we will see that the rejection of Israel was not final. God turned temporarily to the Gentiles and gave them the special responsibility of world evangelization. God had chosen the Jews for this task but they were unfaithful. The Jews were set aside and lost the joy of being God's instruments, but they were not forgotten. In due time they will come back.

In verses 5-8 of this chapter, Paul asks if man's sin gives God an opportunity to demonstrate His faithfulness and mercy, does this mean that sin is good? Paul says this is foolish talk.

Man's Predicament 3:9-18

Paul restates that all people, both Jews and Gentiles, are under the power of sin.

In verses 10b-18 Paul draws from the Old Testament to show man's sinful state and that it is a universal condition. He quotes from Psalms 14:1-3; 5:9; 140:3; 10:7; 36:1; Isaiah 59:7-8. (This was a common method of teaching in Paul's day and was called charaz, which literally means "stringing pearls.")

These Old Testament verses describe three things in the sinful nature:

1. A character with traits of ignorance, indifference, crookedness, and unprofitableness.

2. A tongue whose notes are destructive, deceitful, and malignant.

3. A conduct whose marks are oppression and destruction.

Paul saw the dark side of human nature, but he saw hope beyond.

An old man once said, "My memory is failing, but there are two things I will never forget; that I am a great sinner and that Jesus Christ is a great Savior."

Paul never under-rated the sin of man, and he never under-rated the redeeming power of Jesus. Paul has announced the bad news and now is ready to announce the good news.

The first broad statement in Paul's letter to the Romans is made in chapters 1:18-3:19: **All are sinners.**

The second broad statement is in Romans 3:20-4:25. **All may be saved through faith in Jesus Christ.**

God's Plan 3:19-31

How can a person get into a right relationship with God? This is the greatest question in life. Many new religions have been born in quest of this answer. The Jews said the answer was by the Law. Let us look at God's plan.

It is *God's* plan. 3:21

This is the difference between true Christianity and many new sects and denominations which have arisen. Most religions are man-centered rather than God-centered. They are characterized by false teachings such as salvation through baptism, church attendance, good works, communion, etc. None of these things bring salvation.

God's plan is different. The Bible is the history of God's plan unfolding in the past. His plan is still going on, and it will be concluded in the future. And it is **God's** plan. He sent the prophets. He sent His Son. He provided the sacrifice. He initiates the carrying out of the plan in the lives of individuals.

God's plan is for all. 3:22-24

Eligibility is not gained by wealth, education, or nationality. "All," "anyone," "whoever," are some of the greatest words found in the Bible when related to God's plan to save man.

Salvation is available to Jews and Gentiles on the same terms. It is for anyone who believes that Jesus is the Son of God and claims Him as personal Savior and Lord.

God's plan involves a free gift. 3:24

God's grace is free. It cannot be earned or even deserved, yet it is available for all who will receive it. (John 1:12, Ephesians 2:8-9)

Man-made religion says God's grace can be received *if* a man does something—communion, baptism, etc. God says it is a gift.

A person will act differently because he has received God's gift, but he cannot receive it because of acting differently.

Man is not made right with God by keeping the Law.
3:20,21,28

God's grace is unconditional. If keeping the Law were necessary, then the relationship with God would be conditional.

One of the greatest errors in man's thinking is the idea that if a person keeps the Law, he is a Christian. If this were true, there would be no Christians because no one is able to fully keep the Law. Paul declares:

For we conclude that a person is put right with God only through faith, and not by doing what the Law commands.
Romans 3:28

There is only one plan. 3:23-24

Some say we are all going to Heaven, we are just going by different roads. This thought does not come from a person who is a student of the Bible. Universalism says that eventually everyone will go to Heaven; this is uninformed, wishful thinking.

Some say that in Old Testament days, people were made right with God by keeping the Law. In verse 30 Paul says there has always been only one way, the way of faith. He clearly illustrates this in chapter four.

The result of God's plan is shown in verses 27-31.

Verse 28 shows the result of the plan—right standing with God for those who accept the plan. A by-product is humility on the part of the believer as seen in verse 27.

Humility is a beautiful and desirable quality. It is impossible outside Christianity. Humility requires an unchallengeable dignity. This dignity can come only through a right relationship with God. A truly humble person will know who he is and where he is going because he knows God personally. This makes the peasant to be royalty, a son of the King with full privileges and responsibilities. This person becomes somebody with dignity, yet while robed in the royalty of righteousness he must humbly bow his head and say, "Father God, only because of You can I be who I am."

The great plan brings dignity and humility to everyone who believes. Because of this let us live like ambassadors of the King.

Application and Participation

1. If it is our privilege to be loved by God and receive the promise of eternal life, what is our responsibility?

2. What will happen if we ignore the task God has given us?

3. If all are sinners, does this mean that all need salvation?

4. Name two people you know who need to be saved.

5. Who is responsible for telling them about Christ?

6. If a person can be saved only through faith in Christ, what is the spiritual condition of the person who has "faith" and is depending on baptism to wash away his sin? Will he go to Heaven? Give a Scriptural basis for your answer.

7. How was Moses saved?

8. How would you answer the person who says, "We are all going to Heaven. We all believe in God, we just call Him by different names?"

9. Complete the following sentences.

   In Romans 1:18-3:20 Paul is saying all have _____.

   In Romans 3:21-31 Paul is saying that all who _____ will be saved.

An Illustration of How God Makes a Person Righteous

Outline:

Four Great Truths About How God Makes a Person Righteous, as Seen in Abraham. (Romans 4:1-25)

1. Righteousness Comes by Faith. 4:1-8, 17-22

2. Righteousness Does Not Come through Religious Rituals. 4:9-12

3. Righteousness Is Not Dependent on the Law. 4:13-16

4. Abraham's Way of Faith Is for Everyone. 4:23-25

―――――――――――

Review the first three chapters of Romans.

In chapter 4 Paul gives an illustration of how God makes a person righteous. The Gentiles were not the ones Paul had to convince concerning their sinfulness. His problem was the Jews. For this reason he used Abraham as an example of how God makes a person righteous.

We must remember that Jews thought a person was made right with God through keeping the Law. If Paul could convince them that Abraham was made right with God through faith alone, then the Jews might admit that they too must be saved in the same way.

Why did Paul use Abraham as an illustration?

1. Abraham was the **ideal in the Jewish mind**. Jews honored him as the father of their nation. He was the outstanding Jew of all Jews. They thought he was the pattern of all a person should be. Abraham was a Jewish household name. They could identify with him. It was Abraham who had received the promise to be the father of a great race of people.

2. Paul wanted to show that this new doctrine of being saved by faith was not really new at all; it was as old as Abraham.

3. Abraham was an **outstanding example of one who lived by faith**.

Righteousness Comes by Faith Romans 4:1-8, 17-22

In verses 1 and 2 Paul asks if Abraham was put right with God because of what he did. If so he would have something to boast about. But he had nothing to boast about in God's sight because God knew it was faith rather than works that made Abraham acceptable to Him.

The Scriptures prove that Abraham was not made right through good works or keeping the Law. Paul quoted Genesis 15:6: *Abraham believed God, and because of his faith God accepted him as righteous.* Abraham couldn't have been made right by keeping the Law because God accepted him as righteous long before the Law was given.

How did Abraham act in faith? Where was faith seen in his life?

God called Abraham to leave home, friends, and livelihood and said to him, "If you make this great venture of faith, you will become the father of a great nation." (Genesis 12:1-3) Abraham did not argue or hesitate; he did as God said. He was not sure of all the answers but took each step by faith.

We find a very important account of Abraham's faith in Genesis 15:1-6. God promised Abraham that he would be the father of multitudes. At that time Abraham had not even one child, but he believed the promise. He had faith in God.

In Genesis 18:10 we read of the promise of a son. Isaac was born because of faith. (Genesis 21) Abraham's faith is told of in Hebrews 11:8-19.

Abraham was put right with God because he completely trusted God and took Him at His word. It was not that Abraham had performed the demands of the Law that put him in a special relationship with God; it was his **complete trust in God**.

Paul mentions another great Jewish leader who lived by faith. (Romans 4:6-9) **David** knew the mercy and grace of God. David's sins were many and great, but he came to God in a prayer of faith, believing that God would forgive and accept him. (Psalm 51)

The simple, clear conclusion is that no person is made right by keeping the Law; salvation comes only through faith and trust in God.

27

Where does this leave a person who says he is saved by good works? He is lost without hope until he turns to Christ by faith alone.

Righteousness Does Not Come through Religious Rituals Romans 4:9-12

Certain religious rituals were so important to the Jews that they believed a person's salvation depended on them.

Circumcision was one of these rituals. They thought the man who was not circumcised was not a Jew no matter who his parents were. If a Gentile accepted the Jewish religion, he had to be circumcised.

Concerning Abraham and circumcision, the Jews may say that even if Abraham gained right relationship with God by faith, was he not circumcised? Paul reminds the Jews that Abraham was called and made his commitment of faith **before** he was circumcised.

The account of Abraham's call and commitment is found in Genesis 15:6. The account of his circumcision is found in Genesis 17:10-27.

Abraham was circumcised fourteen years after he had answered God's call. (Romans 4:10) The gateway to right relationship with God was not circumcision; the gateway was faith. Circumcision was the sign and seal that Abraham had already entered into that relationship. (4:11) Paul goes on to state that Abraham is the father of all who believe, whether circumcised or uncircumcised, whether Jew or Gentile. (4:11-12)

Paul is declaring that right standing with God cannot be achieved by an external rite or religious ceremony.

The same principles hold true for present day religions which depend on rituals and ceremonies to make a person right with God. Some new ceremonies have been thought up by man which they say are a part of making a person right with God. These include **infant baptism, communion, church membership,** and other rituals which cannot bring salvation.

One of the most common perversions of the Bible comes when a person says, "I became a Christian when I was baptized." This is like the man who said, "I became a Jew when I was circumcised."

Circumcision for Abraham was a sign or mark saying, "I have committed myself to God by faith."

Baptism for the Christian is a sign or public testimony saying, "By faith I have already received Jesus Christ as my Savior and Lord." Faith in Christ brings the new relationship. Baptism follows as an outward sign of that inward change.

Righteousness Is Not Dependent on the Law
4:13-16

Abraham was accepted as right with God some 400 years before the Law came into existence.

The promises spoken of in verse 13 were based on faith, not on obedience to the Law. God promised that Abraham would be the father or beginning of a new race of people, the chosen

29

people, with the privileges and responsibilities of world re-demption. These promises are seen in Genesis 12:3-7; 13:15-16; 15:1,5,18; 17:8,19 and are mentioned in Acts 3:25 and Gala-tians 3:8. The promises came to Abraham because of his faith in God who made the promises. The promises did not come be-cause of Abraham's good works.

The promise was dependent on two things, the grace of God and the faith of Abraham.

In verses 13-16 Paul speaks of two ways of man getting right with God, but one way is false. The Jews and many people to-day depend on human effort. This is the false way. Paul said the only true way is complete dependence on divine grace. The way of self-effort, trying to be saved by good works, seeks to build the ego of man. It is a natural need for the sinful person to boast of self accomplishment. For this reason religions built on the centrality of man and his works are popular.

Abraham's Way of Faith Is for Everyone 4:23-25

We need to be reminded that we are not saved by keeping the Law. Many people have been so brainwashed by a man-made, self-effort way of salvation that it is difficult for them to fully accept the truth. The truth is God's Word which says that we are made right with God by faith in Jesus Christ. It is faith in the promise of God that whoever believes (has faith) in Him will not perish but will have eternal life.

In conclusion, analyze the following summary statement.

The doctrine of justification by faith means that we are given right standing before God, not through merit, not through the works of the Law, not by ritual or ceremony, but by faith in Him who is our Savior and Lord.

Application and Participation

1. Who is an outstanding Old Testament character who was made right with God by faith?

2. Which came first in the life of Abraham; Law, circumcision, or faith?

3. Where do we find the Old Testament story of Abraham's call? Please give book and chapter.

4. What was the promise made to Abraham?

5. In what way is Abraham's circumcision similar to baptism?

6. Can a person be saved by keeping the Law? Please give a Bible reference.

7. If a person cannot be saved by keeping the Law, what about mixing the Law with faith in order to be saved?

8. What is wrong with the following formula?
Law+faith+baptism=salvation

9. A person is saved by faith in Christ only. What, then, about good works? Does a believer have good works?

10. How is a person made right with God?

ROMANS 5

All Things New in Christ

Outline

1. The New Life 5:1-5

   a. Peace 5:1
   b. Status 5:2
   c. Hope 5:2,5
   d. Joy 5:2-3

2. The God-kind of Love 5:6-11

3. The Second Adam and the New Race 5:12-21

Chapter 5 is a beautiful picture of a man's heart throbbing with the thrill of victory.

Paul gave a gruesome account of man without God in Romans 1:19-3:20. He then in Romans 3:21-31 told how God puts people right with Himself. This way of righteousness by faith is illustrated in chapter 4 with the story of Abraham.

From the valley of sin and death, Paul moves to the mountaintop of walking with God, which is made possible because of Jesus Christ. In Romans 5:1-5 we see the benefits of salvation. In verses 6-11 Paul reminds us again that it was the God-kind of love that could bring mankind into a right relationship with God. Then in verses 12-21 Jesus is introduced as the head of a new humanity.

The New Life 5:1-5

In these verses Paul describes the new life. The basis of this new life is a new faith relationship with Jesus Christ.

◆ The new life is filled with **peace.** 5:1

The greatest need of man is to have peace with God. No man is at peace with himself until he is at peace with God. Many people find it difficult to live with themselves because they have not learned to live in peace with God.

Because of faith the believer is declared righteous in the sight of God. The Christian no longer has to be afraid of God; he is free from God's wrath. The Christian also no longer hates God, but loves Him. This new relationship brings peace.

◆ Because of God's grace, the believer has a new **status.** 5:2

Christ has opened the way for man to come to God. It is almost unbelievable that sinful man could come into the presence of a Holy God and have total peace and joy, but for those who really believe, it is possible.

◆ The new life is filled with **hope.** 5:2,5

One of the outstanding qualities of the Christian is hope. Only the true believer has hope. Hopeless grieving at the death of a loved one does not portray Christianity. Hope does not act like this. The believer can rejoice in troubles and sorrow. (Lamentations 3:21-24)

The Christian is certain to share in the glory of God, beginning in this life and coming to completion in the life to come. What a great hope!

♦ Another quality of the new life is **joy**. 5:2-3

God does not say Christians will escape trials and troubles, but He does say he will be with us through all of them. Rejoicing is a characteristic of those who belong to God. This joy is undimmed by the dark trials through which we pass, and pass through them we will.

A victorious, living church will be a joyful church. A sad, gloomy church will not win unbelievers to Christ.

Because of a new relationship entered into by faith, a new peace comes with joy and hope. This is the result of a new status with God. For these reasons we rejoice.

The God-kind of Love 5:6-11

There are various kinds and qualities of love. There is the kind of human love which would cause a person to die for a friend. But in the death of Jesus a new kind of love was demonstrated. Even while we hated God, He revealed His love for us by sending His Son to die for us. God did not have to do this, but He did. It was Jesus, the Perfect One, dying for sinners. Broken relationships are made right because of Jesus' death. (5:9-10)

Natural human love normally loves the lovable. God's kind of love loves even the unlovable.

Natural human love thinks of what benefits will come if love is shown. God's kind of love is completely centered in others, always more concerned with the welfare of the beloved than with personal gain.

Natural human love is conditional. God loves even while we are sinners. (This does not mean that God loves sin or condones it.)

Because of experiencing the God-kind of love, the believer can learn to love with that kind of love.

The Second Adam and the New Race 5:12-21

In these verses Paul discusses the relation of Christ to mankind. Christ is the head of a new race of people who are called Christians.

Christ is contrasted with Adam. Paul's main objective here was not to discuss Adam or the original sin. His aim was to present Christ as the second Adam, the founder and head of a new humanity.

While it is not the main emphasis of these verses, the universality of sin is again pointed out in verses 12-14. This is linked with the first Adam.

That which is linked with the second Adam is life and joy rather than sin and death.

The disobedience of Adam made all people sinners; the obedience of Christ made it possible for all people to become righteous. Death is a must for all who sin; life is voluntary, dependent on faith in Christ.

People are condemned because of the actions of the first Adam. People may be saved by faith because of the actions of the second Adam.

The hurt and consequences of sin are seen everywhere, but there is hope because Jesus Christ came; He loved, He died, He lives, to give new life to all who fully believe.

We are seeing progressively, chapter after chapter, how God makes a person righteous. It is through a gracious Savior who loved and gave, who lives in the life of each believer. The characteristics of life produced by His indwelling are: peace, security in status, hope, and joy.

Application and Participation

1. How is a person made right with God?

2. From verses 1-5 name two characteristics or qualities of the new life in Christ.

3. Why is joy natural for a believer?

4. How did God show His love for us?

5. What is the difference between natural human love and the love of God?

6. The first Adam brought s _____.
   The second Adam brought s_____.

7. Death was the result of the sin of the first Adam.
   _____ was the result of the second Adam.

8. Jesus came to be the head of a new race of people who voluntarily follow Him. True ___ False ___

9. From the time of Adam's sin all people (except Christ) have sinned, therefore all people need to be saved.
   True ___ False ___

Key verse to memorize: Romans 5:8

Picturesque Answers for Man's Sin Problem

Outline

1. The Answer for Man's Sin Problem Pictured in Baptism
   6:3-14

2. The Answer for Man's Sin Problem Pictured in Slavery
   6:15-23

Introduction to Chapters 6-8

The broken relationship between sinful man and a Holy God is made right by man's acceptance of that which God has done in Jesus Christ. A person enters the Kingdom of God by accepting Christ through faith. Christ is the Savior. By faith a person accepts Him as personal Savior and Lord. (Romans 5:1, John 1:12)

The birth, or beginning, is essential, but God does not desire that His children remain spiritual babies. While the new birth may be called regeneration, the growth and development may be called sanctification.

Remember the theme of Romans: How God makes a person righteous.

From Romans 3:21 to 5:21 we see how God brings a person into right standing with Himself. It is by faith. Now in chapters 6, 7, and 8 Paul tells how a person can be sanctified—how righteousness can reign in the life of a Christian.

Since sanctification is the theme of the next three chapters, it will be good if we understand a basic definition of the word.

Sanctification is growing toward sinlessness. It is not perfection.

Sanctification means to be set apart or separated from. It is to be set apart *from* the things of the world and set apart *for* the work of God. This is an on-going, growing experience. A person is sanctified when he is born again. He is set apart or dedicated to the purpose and service of God by the conversion experience. But that is only the beginning of a daily process wherein the believer becomes more righteous, more holy, more like Jesus.

The Bible teaches that Christ not only frees us from the penalty of sin as seen in Romans 5; He also frees us from the power of sin. This is the main topic of discussion in chapters 6, 7, and 8.

The main obstacle to the reign of righteousness in the believer is sin.

The key to the reign of righteousness in the believer is a faith relationship with the living Christ.

Romans 5:10 says, *We were God's enemies, but he made us his friends through the death of his Son. Now that we are God's friends, how much more will we be saved by Christ's life!*

39

It is one-sided to emphasize only the death of Christ. By His death, sacrifice was made to enable God to accept people in a new father-child relationship. But this new relationship is sustained by the Christ who lives—even in our hearts.

Chapter 6 is better understood if we begin with verse 20 of chapter 5. We can better understand the subject of sin if we understand its relationship to the Law. Many sincere people who call themselves Christians are lost because they wrongly relate the Law to sin. Most of these people have tried to make the Law, or the keeping of the Law, to be their savior.

Paul says in Romans 5:20-21 that the Law brought to man a consciousness of sin. Because of the Law, man learns that he is a sinner. The Law reveals the source of our problems. The source is sin. The Savior is Christ.

We need to remember that the Law did not produce sin and that it cannot remove sin. The Law reveals the fact of sin in order that we might find the cure. The cure is seen in 5:21.

In light of the grace of God, is it all right for a person to continue in sin so that God's grace will be more greatly displayed? Paul says no, certainly not.

The Answer for Man's Sin Problem Pictured in Baptism 6:3-14

Paul reminds the believers of their relationship to sin as portrayed in baptism.

In these verses, baptism is seen as a symbolic act. When a believer goes down into the water, it is a picture of burial. This portrays the burial of the old sinful nature. We must remember that a symbol or picture is not the real thing. A picture of a man is not a man. The man was a reality before the picture was possible. If baptism pictures burial, there must have been a death before the picture is possible. The death occurred when the person repented of his sins and accepted Christ as Savior. There was a death to the old sinful nature which ruled before salvation came.

Baptism is a symbol or picture of that death. The death came before the act of baptism. If the symbol is to be true, baptism must be by immersion. Sprinkling can never portray a burial. To change the picture will eventually alter the idea behind the picture. This may be the reason many religious groups have little emphasis on the need to be born again by faith in Christ. The picture of sprinkling does not adequately portray the conversion experience.

Not only does baptism picture a death and burial of the old nature; it goes further to picture a resurrection to new life. This is pictured as the person is raised up out of the "grave" of baptism—raised to share in the new life of a living Lord.

Please remember again, the resurrection does not occur when a person is baptized. This is a picture or symbol of something that has already happened. It happened when the person repented of his sin, died to the old way of life, and accepted the new life offered by Christ.

Baptism, then, is an external picture of an internal experience. The internal experience must have happened before the time of baptism in order to have anything to picture.

One word may be used to describe the entire picture; union. The hope of the believer is union with Christ—the believer living in Christ and Christ living in the believer. Because of this union, which is pictured in baptism, sin can no longer rule over our lives. The death and resurrection, as experienced in salvation and pictured in baptism, bring a completely new life style. (6:12-14)

The Answer to Man's Sin Problem Pictured in Slavery 6:15-23

This new life style is characterized by slavery to righteousness.

To yield yourself to someone means you become his servant. Paul says a person can become a servant of sin, which leads to destruction and death. But Christ came to free man from slavery to sin, to become a slave to righteousness which leads to constructiveness and eternal life. The choice belongs to every person.

Many people choose sin rather than the power which is able to set them free. Each person has the choice of self-deception or self-honesty. Unbelief keeps a person from God. God has solved the problem of sin, but man's unbelief in this way of deliverance separates him from God.

The choice of believing involves entering a voluntary slavery. Usually a slave is a slave because of external pressures which he cannot resist. God accepts only people who become voluntary slaves to righteousness. However, a person does not decide to become a slave on his own initiative; he decides in response to God's call.

How does a person become a slave to Jesus Christ and righteousness?

In the inner life there is a citadel (a strong hold, a fortress) which is not changed by external pressures or self-will. A person may free himself of many things, but the citadel does not give up self because it is the very being of the person. It is the ego, the self.

But when a person sees the glory of Christ, the inner citadel is captivated by this Person. Christ is so beautiful that a person wants to yield everything—his very self—to the command of Christ. To never have had this slavery to Christ is to have never lived.

This is costly. All barriers must be broken down. One must see in the Scriptures the person of Christ and receive Him as personal Savior and Lord. The sinful self is diminished and Christ is enthroned.

Whatever captures your imagination will eventually capture your will. When will and imagination are together, a person will be strong.

No man has been free who has not been enslaved by something great.

Paul had the answer for the sin problem. A person can know and experience the answer. It is pictured in baptism and slavery —union with the living Christ.

Application and Participation

1. Define sanctification.

2. What is the key obstacle to the reign of righteousness in the believer?

3. For the believer the Law: a. Reveals ___ b. Saves ___

4. In chapter 6 Paul speaks of:
   a. Baptism ___
   b. The Lord's Supper ___

5. Why and how did Paul use baptism to illustrate man's relationship to sin?

6. Why is sprinkling not an acceptable method of baptism?

7. Baptism is an external picture of an internal change.
   True ___   False ___

8. If a person is a slave to Christ, it means that person is weak and powerless. True ___   False ___

9. How does a person become a slave to Jesus Christ?

10. How will my daily life be affected if I am a slave to Jesus Christ?

11. Analyze and discuss the following statement: "No man has been free who has not been enslaved by something great."

Key verse to memorize: Romans 6:8

ROMANS 7

Righteousness Developed

Outline

1. Righteousness Developed in the Believer through a New Relationship 7:1-6

2. Righteousness Developed in the Believer through a Right Understanding of the Relationship Between Law and Sin 7:7-13

3. Righteousness Developed in the Believer through Victory Over Self 7:14-25

The theme we have chosen to develop in the letter to the Romans is: **How God makes a person righteous**.

The theme in chapter 3:21 through chapter 5 is how God brings a person into right standing with Himself. The emphasis is on God making the person righteous. A summary statement is found in Romans 5:1: *Now that we have been put right with God through faith, we have peace with God through our Lord Jesus Christ.*

The natural human tendency is to try to earn salvation. This was true in Paul's day as well as today. Most religions have a man-made system of required works to be done by a person in order to be saved.

To understand Paul's position, read his letters to the Galatians and to the Romans. Paul dogmatically proclaims that only because of the free grace of God can a person be saved. Even man's ability to have faith in Christ comes from God. Therefore no person can boast of any human accomplishment which has produced his right standing with God.

As we remember from the study of chapter 6, Paul turns to the subject of how a person matures or develops in the Christian life. This development, of course, can take place only after one is justified, put right with God through faith. The development is called sanctification. Sanctification for the believer is a process wherein he becomes more like Christ. It is a gradual development where the command *Let this mind be in you which was in Christ Jesus,* (Philippians 2:5) becomes a reality.

Many face the danger of beginning the Christian life by faith in Christ and then changing to a works program for developing as a Christian.

Let us repeat—man enters the Christian life by faith; he continues to develop because of a faith relationship to Christ. Through this faith relationship a person is born again and continues to develop toward Christ-likeness. The believer is both justified and sanctified by a faith relationship to Jesus Christ.

The emphasis of chapters 6, 7, and 8 is how God sanctifies a sinful person.

Before reading chapter 7, notice the last verse in chapter 6. *For sin pays its wage—death; but God's free gift is eternal life in union with Christ Jesus our Lord.*

A key phrase in this verse which introduces us to chapter 7 is "in union with Christ Jesus."

Righteousness Developed in the Believer through a New Relationship 7:1-6

Paul uses the laws governing marriage to illustrate the new relationship to Christ. He says it is important that the husband be dead before the wife can marry again. If a woman marries another man when her husband is living, she commits adultery.

Paul is saying there must be a death when a person enters into a relationship with Christ. The law did not die, but in verse 4, *You also have died, as far as the Law is concerned.* In this death, a person is set "free from the Law." (6:6)

To try to live by the Law and by faith in Christ at the same time is to commit spiritual adultery. Paul wrote the entire letter to the Galatians to refute the idea of salvation gained through the Law and faith.

The normal, human-centered approach to gaining right standing with God is seen in a struggle to keep the Law. This is a rewards-punishment relationship.

God's way of giving a person right standing is through a personal relationship. It is union with Christ; Christ in me and I in Christ.

There must be a break with the rewards-punishment relationship before entering a personal faith relationship with Christ. If the break is not made, spiritual adultery will result.

Creative energy comes from grace, not from the Law. A person is set free by the grace of God. He is set free from the bondage of the Law.

Righteousness Developed in the Believer through a Right Understanding of the Relationship Between the Law and Sin 7:7-13

◆The Law of God is good and right. 7:12
◆The purpose of the Law is to point out sin. 7:7
◆The Law was not given to forgive or remove sin.
◆The Law makes sin appear as sin.
◆There is nothing wrong with the Law; the wrong is in the heart of man.

Paul does not discard the Law as a moral guide. He does not say that the Christian is not under obligation to obey the Law. He emphasized the true function of the Law as the revealer of sin.

Throughout his writings Paul states that righteousness can never be the product of the Law.

The believer is not imprisoned by the Law as a slave to keeping the Law. A believer does not ignore the Law, but goes much further; he lives by the law of the Spirit.

Righteousness Developed in the Believer through Victory Over Self 7:14-25

A strange, yet common experience to every believer is the civil war raging inside himself. After a person has been born again he has two natures. There is a constant struggle between these two natures. One nature wants to be righteous while the other seeks unrighteousness.

God makes a person righteous as He gives victory over the old nature.

Paul said, "I know what is right and I want to do right, yet I do not do it. I know what is wrong and I don't want to do it, yet I do the wrong." This is a feeling experienced by every believer. The struggle is not bad; it is a sign of life. When the struggle ceases, beware! It is frustrating and sometimes disappointing, but we have hope because it is God who is working in us to bring about full righteousness.

From one point of view this passage might be called a demonstration of inadequacies.

1. It demonstrates the inadequacy of human knowledge. If to know the right thing was to do the right thing, then life would be easy. But knowledge by itself does not make a good man.

2. It demonstrates the limitations of diagnosis. Paul knew quite clearly what was wrong; but he was quite unable to put it right.

A helpful key in understanding this obstacle of becoming righteous is to count the number of times a personal pronoun appears in these twelve verses. No less than forty times the words, "I," "me," or "my" occur.

The struggle is between the old self-centered self and the new self God wants us to become.

The answer for victory is seen in verse 25. Jesus Christ living daily in our lives will bring change and victory.

Application and Participation

1. A major theme of chapters 6-8 is:
   a. Second coming ___
   b. Sanctification ___

2. What human relationship does Paul use to illustrate the new faith relationship to Christ?

3. How can a person commit spiritual adultery?

4. According to Paul in chapter 7, "We are free from the Law." True ___ False ___

5. What is the purpose of the Law?

6. A person is made righteous by keeping the Law. True ___ False ___

7. How is the Law related to sin?

8. Describe the struggle in the heart of the believer.

9. To know the right thing means that a person will do the right thing. True ____ False ____

10. Righteousness comes by keeping the Law. True ____ False ____

11. Righteousness comes only through _____ in Christ.

Key verses to memorize: Romans 7:24-25

ROMANS 8

Life in the Spirit

Outline

Four Great Characteristics of Life in the Spirit

1. Full Pardon 8:1-11
   a. Freedom from Reign of Sin and Death 8:2-4
   b. Freedom from Life of Old Nature 8:5-8
   c. Freedom to Let the Spirit of Christ Live in Our Lives 8:9-11

2. Obligation: 8:12-17
   a. To Live a Righteous Life 8:12-13
   b. To Live As God's Sons 8:14-16
   c. To Live As Good Stewards 8:17

3. Assurance: 8:18-30
   a. Of Future Glory 8:18-25
   b. Of the Holy Spirit's Help in Prayer 8:26-27
   c. On God's Control of His Purpose and Plans for His Children 8:31-32

4. Eternal Security: 8:31-39
   a. Because God Is for Us 8:31-32
   b. Because God Declares Us Not Guilty 8:33-34
   c. Because Nothing Can Separate Us from the Love of God 8:35-39

In the letter to the Christians at Rome, Paul climbs several mountains, moving from the valley of despair to the mountain top of victory.

The first of these mountain tops is seen in Chapter 5:1-11. The first 4 chapters are the valley of despair as man in his sinful condition is portrayed. Paul begins climbing the mountain in chapter 3:21 with God's plan to save man. He climbs higher in chapter 4 in illustrating how salvation is attained in the example of Abraham. And then as if on a mountain top for the whole world to hear, Paul exclaims, "*Now that we have been put right with God through faith, we have peace with God through our Lord Jesus Christ.*" (5:1)

Paul then walks down from the mountain into the valley of human struggle—the struggle to become righteous in daily living. Chapters 6 and 7 deal with the sin problem. Until the last part of chapter 7, Paul seems as if he might break into a million pieces in the fierce struggle with sin. He says, "*Oh, what a terrible predicament I'm in! Who will free me from my slavery to this deadly lower nature?*" (7:24)

Then the mountain top is again reached with the shout of freedom, "*Thank God! It has been done by Jesus Christ our Lord. He has set me free.*" (7:25)

The entire eighth chapter is a victorious mountain top experience. (The third mountain top, climatic point is chapter 12.) Each of the mountain top exclamations begins with "therefore" or "now."

Let us examine more closely this great well-known chapter 8. It is a chapter of music in the heart of a man living in the Spirit. It is a chapter of freedom ringing in the heart of a slave. It is a chapter of victory for the "chiefest of sinners"—you and me.

Without attempting to exhaust every teaching in the chapter, let us note some great highlights.

Remember the theme of Romans: "How God makes a person righteous."

In general there are three aspects of the process in which a person is made righteous as seen in Romans. They are:

1. **Forgiveness** (3:21- chapter 5)
2. **Cleansing from the pollution of sin** (chapters 6-8)
3. **Infusion of the Divine life** (chapter 12)

The second aspect, "cleansing from the pollution of sin," finds the ultimate answer in chapter 8. That answer is living in the Spirit and the living of the Spirit in the believer. It is nothing less than union with Christ.

Note four characteristics of life in the Spirit.

Full Pardon 8:1-11

There is no condemnation. (8:1) For the prisoner of sin sentenced to die, this is good news. The Law could only condemn sinful humanity, but God paid the ransom to gain full pardon and set the condemned free. (8:3) God paid the ultimate price by giving His only Son to become the necessary sacrifice to for the freedom of man.

The first realization in the heart of the new believer is the feeling of freedom.

♦ There is the freedom from the principle of the law of sin and death. (8:2)

This law or principle is broken. Under bondage to the law of sin and death, the more you sin the more you are bound. The pleasure becomes less but the necessity is greater. This is changed in the believer when a new principle/law takes over. A believer's attitudes toward sin change. There is a new hatred of sin. We may call this new principle the obedience-to-God principle. The new principle brings pleasure and satisfaction which the believer loves more than the pleasure of sin.

The old principle is self-centered. The new principle is God-centered. These two principles are found in verses 5-11.

♦ There is freedom to let the Spirit of Christ live in our lives. (8:9-11)

This new principle is none other than Christ living in us. When this freedom is exercised, God has right of way to the final say; He is the authority in our lives.

The same Spirit who raised Christ from death lives in the believer. It is thrilling to know that the same power that raised Jesus is working in our lives to make us righteous.

Obligation (8:12-17)

In verse 12, *So then, my brothers, we have an obligation.* One of the greatest perversions of Christian thought is the idea of being saved to go to heaven and forgetting the obligations the new life brings.

◆ We are obligated to live a righteous life. (8:12-13)

The Christian lives the Christian life. The person who does not live the Christian life is not a Christian. When a person is saved, his life changes. The old habits of the world are not to be a normal part of the Christian's life.

Today's immorality indicates that we are not living in a Christian nation. When God has touched the heart, new words come from a person's mouth. Filthy curse words will disappear from a person's vocabulary when Christ lives inside.

◆ We are obligated to live as God's sons. (8:14-16)

As sons we are not afraid of the Father. A son partakes of the core of the nature and character of the Father. A son is motivated by love rather than fear. He does the same things the Father does and does them for the same reason. A son gets the same joy out of doing something that God gets from doing it. The greatest difference between the spirit of sons and the spirit of servitude is the presence of joy in the spirit of sons. The son will be motivated by joy. A servant is motivated by praise and fear.

In the process of becoming righteous, the more a person lives under the spirit of sonship, the more he will be free from sin.

Praise to the son will bring humility. Praise to the servant will bring pride.

◆ As God's sons we are obligated to be good stewards. (8:17)

We are responsible to God for the way we use everything we have because God owns everything.

A steward is a person who is in charge of something which belongs to someone else. God is concerned about what we do with our bodies, our talents, our money, our fields—wait, did I say "our...?" Remember all these are His possessions and we are temporary stewards.

Assurance 8:18-30

This section may well be called "A glorious hope." It is this hope that gives assurance to our lives.

◆ We have assurance because of the hope of future final victory when we will share in the glory of Christ. (8:18-25)

We have the assurance that even nature will be redeemed from the presence and power of sin.

This passage tells us something of the terrible power of sin. The coming of sin brought reverberations to the entire creation. Ever since, nature has been longing for the overthrow of this unnaturalness brought by sin.

The believer can face trials and persecutions because he knows that the things suffered now cannot be compared with the glory that is going to be revealed to us. (8:18)

◆ We are assured of the Holy Spirit's help in our prayer life. (8:26-27)

The Holy Spirit helps us do that which we cannot do for ourselves.

Sometimes things are so bad we don't know how to pray. Sometimes we don't know the right requests to make. Sometimes our joy may be so great that human words are not adequate to express our feelings to God.

In all these times the Holy Spirit helps us to know how to pray.

◆ We have assurance that God is in full control of His purpose and plans. (8:28-30)

In suffering and weakness, in persecution or hardship, in everything, God is in control. For those who love Him and have a sense of His call and are committed to His purpose, He makes "all things work together for good."

We must remember that it is God who makes all things work to gether for good. He can turn sickness and misfortune, hardship and persecution, sorrow and death—everything we experience—into channels of blessing.

The purpose of God is that the sons of God shall be like the Son of God. (8:29) We have assurance that those whom God called, He made righteous and He will share His glory with them. (8:30)

Eternal security 8:31-39

In these final verses Paul rises to a peak of overflowing joy and praise. In the first chapters he has led us from the depths of man's sin, of man's rebellion against God. Now the picture is completely changed, showing us the new relationship of God and man which is sealed for eternity. Nothing can separate us from the love of God. This leads us to the thrilling fact of eternal security of the believer.

♦ Eternal security is a fact because God is for us. (8:31-32)

If God is for us, who can be against us? When life gets rough and it seems all our friends turn their backs, when neighbors laugh at our "new religion," do you know who is "for us?" It is God himself. If you seem to be in the minority, remember that God and you make a majority.

God showed that He is for us when He gave His Son.

♦ Eternal security is a fact for the believer because God has declared us not guilty. (8:33-34)

So what if someone condemns you for following Christ; God Himself declares you not guilty. (8:33)

Who can condemn you? No one—because the only true Judge says you are not guilty—based on what Jesus did on the cross to free you. (8:34)

♦ We have eternal security because *nothing can separate us from the Love of God.* (8:35-39)

Paul gives a list of great trials: tribulation, distress, persecution, famine, nakedness, peril, and sword.

Christians through the years have endured these trials. No trial or hardship is able to separate us from the love of Christ. They

59

may separate us from wealth and health, from family and friends, and from comfort. But they cannot separate us from the love of God.

God's love is unchangeable.
God's love is unconditional.
God's love is eternal.

God's love often reveals itself in the "crosses" of affliction and hardships—even death. Remember Calvary. God paid such a price to show His love to and for us. This love is enduring, lasting, eternal. To have this love means eternal security because the Lover, God Himself, says so.

Application and Participation

1. A person is set free by obeying the Law.
   True ____ False ____

2. Chapter 8 of Romans could be entitled
   Life in the Spirit ____
   New Birth ____

3. The Holy Spirit lives in the heart of the believer.
   True ____ False ____

4. What is the difference between the spirit of sonship and the spirit of a slave?

5. _____ has been affected by sin and groans to be free.

6. Who helps us to know how to pray?

60

7. Chapter 8 gives a hopeless picture for the believer.
   True ___ False ___

8. Name at least two things found in this chapter that cannot separate us from the love of God.

9. Why can the believer be sure that once he is saved he will always be saved?

10. Please analyze and discuss the following statement.
   "Love God with all your heart and do as you please."

Key verses to memorize: Romans 8:8,38-39

ROMANS 9

God's Sovereign Freedom

Outline

1. Paul Expresses Concern about Spiritual Condition of Fellow Jews 9:1-5

2. God's Way of Salvation in Past and Present—His Sovereign Grace 9:6-18

3. God's Mercy to Those Deserving Judgment—Both Gentiles and Jews 9:19-29

4. The Jews Searching for Salvation through Law 9:30-33

After a great mountain top experience related in chapter 8, Paul in a sense, pauses to deal with a problem. The problem concerned the place of the Jews in God's eternal purpose. Paul deals with this in chapters 9, 10, and 11. Some possible titles for this three-chapter section are: "Election," "God's Purpose in History," or "The Problem of the Jews."

Some other major teachings found in these chapters are: the sovereignty of God, the free will of man, predestination, and of course, God's way of making a person righteous.

omans 9-11 is both separate from, and at the same time, related to the rest of the book. These chapters tell how God has made people righteous—in the past among the Jews, now among the Gentiles, and in the future among the Jews.

hese three chapters could be studied in one lesson, but in order to make a closer study of the chapters, we will study them separately. Let us look more closely now at chapter 9.

aul emphasizes the sovereign freedom of God in this chapter.

Paul Expresses Concern about the Spiritual Condition of Fellow Jews 9:1-5

aul had just concluded the great chapter 8 in which he dealt with freedom and security. Even in his thrill of victory, he could not forget those living in defeat and death—his people, the ews.

nowing his fellow Jews were a lost, doomed people made Paul ad, so much so that he said he would gladly give up his relationship with Christ if it would help them. Paul did not give up his relationship to Christ, but he did give his life in his effort to make the Gospel known to the Jews.

ow much do we care about our fellow countrymen who are on he way to hell?

n verses 4 and 5 Paul tells of the advantages of the Jews.

. They were **chosen**, the children of God.
. They had the **glory** of God, yet had rejected Him.

3. They had the **covenants**. God had renewed His covenant with the Jews again and again.
4. They had the **Law**.
5. They had the **true worship**. This refers to the worship in the Temple.
6. They had the **promises**.
7. They had the **fathers**. They had the heritage from the patriarchs, Abraham, Isaac, and Jacob.
8. The promised **Messiah** was a Jew.

God's Way of Salvation in Past and Present— His Sovereign Grace 9:6-18

This is the meaning of the Bible teaching about predestination and election. When a believer traces the roots of his salvation, he is always led back to the eternal grace of God.

Paul faces the question, Has God's promise to Israel failed? He answers the question in verses 6-13. He shows that the promise is according to election. First, Paul says that not everyone born a Jew is a true Jew. He then illustrates this by citing some Jewish history. No one can say that God is unjust because chosen people reject Him.

Two great truths shown in chapters 9-11 are the sovereignty of God and the free will of man. Both are true facts that we as humans cannot understand.

Regarding the sovereign power of God, verses 15-16 are clear. *So then, it does not depend on what man wants or does, but on on God's mercy.* Verse 18 also says, *So then, God has mercy on whom he wishes, and he makes stubborn whom he wishes.*

Salvation of man in the Old Testament was dependent upon God's sovereign grace. Salvation today depends on God's sovereign grace. From these verses we conclude that God is truly God.

God's Mercy to Those Deserving Judgment— Both Gentiles and Jews 9:19-29

Verse 22 is a key verse in this section.

In the preceding verses, Paul illustrated how God had selected some and not others. The objection arises in verse 19; if God selected some, how can those whom God did not select be held responsible? Does the fault belong to God who is all powerful? Paul's answer is very strong. He says that no man has the right to argue with God.

The potter and the clay is used to illustrate a truth. As the potter has the right to shape the clay as he pleases, so does God have a right to shape men's lives as he chooses. No one has the right to question God's way of doing things.

God does not make men lost.

Verses 22-24 tell us that God dealt with lost men in patience and mercy, extending his grace even to the Gentiles.

The Jews Searching for Salvation through Law 9:30-33

In general there are two views regarding the way of salvation. Both views are seen in these verses.

There was the Jewish way, the mistaken way. Jews tried to make themselves right with God by strict obedience to the Law. This was a salvation to be earned by doing good works. The Jews worked hard; they were serious in their search for salvation. Paul's conclusion is seen in verse 31. In all their search and keeping of the laws, the Jews never found a law that could save them.

Verse 32 says it is fatal to base our hope on works. Good works will not unlock heaven's door for Jews nor Gentiles.

Then there was the true view regarding salvation. The answer to the sin problem of both Jew and Gentile is found in verse 30; *...not trying to put themselves right with God, were put right with Him through faith.*

A large majority of "Christians" (not true Christians) today are in the same situation as the Jews. The mistake is the same and the fate is the same. Strict obedience to a set of church rules and laws leaves a person religious but lost.

The constant message of the Bible is that no man is put right with God by doing good works. Salvation comes only by faith in Christ alone.

Chapter 10 will continue with the reason for Israel's rejection.

Application and Participation

1. What was Paul's feeling about the Jews as seen in Romans 9:1-3?

2. In Romans 9:4-9, Paul gives at least eight privileges the Jews had. Name as many as you can.

66

3. Choose the doctrines which are found in chapter 9.
   Election, sovereignty of God, second coming, baptism,
   God's purpose, God's mercy, salvation by faith, communion
   (Underline 5 only.)

4. Paul was wrong in becoming emotionally upset about the
   lost condition of Israel. True ___ False ___

5. God has the right and the power to do as he pleases.
   True ___ False ___

6. If God is all powerful (sovereign) does man have a freedom
   of whether to trust God?

7. Some are elected or chosen by God. God's election depends
   on what man wants or does. (8:16) True ___ False ___

8. God shows His mercy only to those who deserve it.
   True ___ False ___

9. What truth does the illustration of the potter and the clay
   teach?

10. As found in this chapter, what was the problem of the Jews?
    Or why were they rejected?

11. A "stumbling stone" is mentioned in verse 32. Who was the
    stumbling stone?

12. In what way was He a stumbling stone?

God's Plan Of Salvation

Outline

1. God's Plan of Salvation 10:1-13

    a. God's plan demands devotion based on true knowledge. 10:2

    b. God's plan excludes man's righteousness. 10:3-4

    c. God's plan is based on faith. 10:6-13

    d. God's plan is **God's** plan, designed and completed by God. 10:6-8

    e. In God's plan, salvation is available to all. 10:11,13

    f. God's plan is the same for all people. 10:8,11-13

2. God's Plan Offered to Israel but Rejected 10:14-21

In chapter 9 we saw the sovereignty of God. In chapter 10 we see man's responsibility. People who reject Christ are responsible for their own lostness.

The major theme of chapter 10 is that **Israel is responsible for her lost condition because she rejected the message of faith**.

Paul begins chapter 10 much as he did chapter 9. His words were strong as he pointed out the unbelief of the Jews in chapter 9. As he begins chapter 10, he speaks tenderly with love and compassion. (10:1) He is delivering a hard message to people he loves. Paul desired more than anything else that his people, the Jews, would be saved. He cared for them. He prayed for them.

We need to realize that some truths may not be popular, but every preacher is called to preach the truth, no matter how unpopular or unpleasant. No preacher should enjoy preaching the truth about hell, but every God-directed preacher must preach it.

When preaching against sin and unrighteousness, the preacher's heart should reflect the attitude of Paul—love and compassion.

Paul could easily identify with the Jews because he had walked the same road of trying to earn salvation by keeping the Law. (See Philippians 3.) He was more devoted and zealous than any other Jew, yet he was not a Christian until his experience with Christ on the Damascus road.

God's Plan of Salvation 10:1-13

✦ **God's plan demands devotion based on true knowledge.** 10:2

It is not enough to be enthusiastic. A person may have a misguided enthusiasm. Many people are serious, but it takes more than seriousness to go to heaven. A communist or atheist may be serious, zealous, enthusiastic, but certainly is not a child of God.

A person may be devoted to his religion to the point of fanaticism, yet if that devotion is based on error, he is not a Christian. This was the condition of the Jews.

People around the world have a natural desire to gain favor with God and are searching for ways to achieve that purpose. They, like the Jews, have not known by experience the way in which God puts people right with Himself. The problem for the Jews was not that their God was false; it was ignorance of God's plan of salvation.

The major religions of the world fall, to some extent, into the same error that the Jews made. This mistake is not only that people have not known the true way of salvation, but have tried to set up their own way. (10:3)

True knowledge comes from the Bible, not from man's words about God's Word. True knowledge is God's words illuminated by the Holy Spirit and received by the believer.

♦ God's plan of salvation excludes man's righteousness. 10:3-4

There is God's righteousness which is given to man and there is man's righteousness brought about by much self-effort. The first is true righteousness. The second is a false righteousness which Isaiah speaks of when he says, "Man's righteousness is as filthy rags." (Isaiah 64:6) Both the righteousness of God and the righteousness of man are seen in verses 3 and 4. One is described in verse 3 ...*and have tried to set up their own way.* The other is described in verse 4, *Everyone who believes is put right with God.*

Note in verse 4, *For Christ has brought the Law to an end...* "End" may be interpreted in two ways. One is that the Law came to an end with the coming of Christ. The other is that Christ was the end or fulfillment of the Law.

◆ **God's plan of salvation is based on faith.** 10:6-13

*Everyone who **believes** is put right with God.* 10:4
*...the message of **faith**.* 10:8
*...**believe** in your heart.* 10:9
*For we **believe** in our hearts...* 10:10
*Whoever **believes** in him...* 10:11
Without faith it is impossible to please God. Hebrews 11:6

Trying to mix faith with the Law brings the eternal curse of God. (See chapter one of Galatians.)

The Jews just could not think it possible to be made righteous by simply accepting by faith that which Christ provided on the cross. It was the rejection of this message of faith that caused God to set aside the Jewish nation for awhile and turn His attention to the Gentiles.

God's plan is based on faith, from the point of being saved to the ultimate sanctification.

◆ **God's plan is *God's* plan, designed and completed by God.** 10:6-8

In these verses Paul quotes Deuteronomy 30:12-13. He is saying it is not our effort that brought Christ into the world or raised Him from the dead. It is not our good works that bring about righteousness. It has been done for us, and we have only to accept it as a gift. It was finished on the cross.

Hear Jesus say in John 19:30, *"It is finished!"* God gave His all. There was no more to give. Man must receive by faith what God has already completed.

71

♦ In God's plan, salvation is available to everyone. 10:11,13

The Jews felt themselves to be special. They found it difficult to believe that God's plan included **everyone.**

God's invitation goes to the poor and the rich alike. It goes to the uneducated and the educated. God's invitation ...*includes everyone, for there is no difference between Jews and Gentiles; God is the same Lord of all, and richly blesses all who call on him.* 10:12

Everyone who calls on the name of the Lord will be saved. 10:13

It is for anybody, all, everyone, anyone who will believe and follow Christ.

♦ God's plan is the same for all people. 10:8,11-13

Often people who are ignorant of the Bible will say, "We are all going to heaven, just on different roads." These verses in chapter 10 tell us that only those who act in faith based on true knowledge can be right with God.

There are **not** many ways to be saved; there is **only one way.** If there were many ways, it would not have been necessary for Jesus to die the agonizing death on the cross.

Let us look more closely at verses 9 and 10. These verses are well-known for their clear, simple picture of how a person can be saved.

To be in right standing with God, a person must:

1. Say that Jesus Christ is Lord.

The Greek word for Lord is "Kurios." This was a key word for the early Christians. To call Jesus "Lord" was to rank Him with the Emperor and with God. It meant giving Him first place in all of life.

2. Believe that Jesus is risen from the dead.

The resurrection is the key to Christian belief. The Christian must believe that Jesus **lived**, but also that Jesus **lives**. The Christian must know **about** Christ, but he also must **know** Christ. He must know the **sacrifice** of Christ, but also the **conquest** of Christ. The Christian must know Christ the **martyr**, and also Christ the **victor**.

3. Confess with his lips.

Belief is empty without confession. Confession is giving witness before men. Not only God, but our fellowmen, must know that we are Christians. A person must declare to men what side he is on.

God's Plan Offered to Jews but Rejected 10:14-21

The often quoted verses 14-17 are usually used to show our missionary responsibility. In order to be saved, people must hear. In order to hear, people need a preacher.

Verse 18 indicates Paul's purpose in these verses when he said, *But I ask, have they not heard? Indeed they have.* He was showing that Israel had heard but had not accepted the message of faith.

The message of Isaiah's generation was still true in Paul's day, *All day long I held out my hands to welcome a disobedient and rebellious people.* 10:21

The Jews were lost, not because God made them lost, but because they rejected God's invitation.

Application and Participation

1. If a truth is unpopular, it is best to avoid preaching on the subject. True ____ False ____

2. When preaching that people are sinners and lost, the preacher should be filled with: joy, sorrow, bitterness, love. (Choose only two)

3. Please interpret verse 4, *For Christ has brought the Law to an end, so that everyone who believes is put right with God.*

4. What was the mistake of the Jews?

5. Give two verses in chapter 10 which are most often used to lead a person to Christ.

6. According to this chapter the only difference between the Jew and the Gentile is: The Jew is saved by the Law and the Gentile is saved by faith. True ____ False ____

7. How would you respond to the statement, "We are all going to heaven, we are only going by different roads?"

8. Israel had the opportunity to hear the message of faith.
   True ___ False ___

9. Paul quotes from the Old Testament in this chapter. Name one Old Testament character whom Paul quotes.

10. When Israel rejected the message of faith, God turned his attention to the _____.

Key verses to memorize: Romans 10:9,10,11.

ROMANS 11

The Jews in God's Plan of the Ages

Outline

1. The Redeemed Remnant 11:1-10

2. The Salvation of the Gentiles 11:11-24

3. The Hope of Israel 11:25-32

4. Song of Praise 11:33-36

In chapter 9 Paul tells of the Jews' failure to respond to the love of God. In this chapter it is also pointed out that the unbelief of the Jews did not mean the failure of God's promise to Abraham. In the matter of salvation, God is sovereign and elects whoever He wills to be saved.

In chapter 10 the responsibility for failing to respond to the message of faith was placed completely upon Israel. It was Israel's rejection of the one way of salvation—faith—which caused God to reject her.

Now we come to the final chapter in this section concerning the Jews' relationship with God. It had seemed that Israel had been completely excluded from the mercy of God. In chapter 11 Paul clarifies the matter and assures the Jews of hope—hope which still must come through faith.

The Redeemed Remnant 11:1-10

God's rejection of Israel is neither total nor final; it is partial and temporary. There was the remnant from the days of Abraham until the days of Paul, and even until today. To illustrate that God had not rejected every Jew, Paul speaks of himself. He said in essence, "I am a Jew and God has chosen me. This shows that not every Jew has been excluded from the mercy of God." (11:1-2) Some Jews are saved, therefore one cannot say that God has predestined that all be lost.

Another illustration is used from the Old Testament. (11:2-4) At one time Elijah thought he was the only Israelite who remained faithful to God. God answered him, *I have kept for myself seven thousand men who have not worshipped the false God Baal.* 11:4

Thus, into the Jewish thought came the idea of the **remnant**. The prophets began to see that there had never been a time, and there would never be a time when every Jew in the Israelite nation was true to God.

The idea of the remnant also meant that a part of the whole would always be true to God. Especially was this idea strong in the life of Isaiah. He called his son Shear-Jashub, which means "the salvation of the remnant."

This teaches us that God does not save people in groups or nations, but as individuals. The relationship of faith is an individual relationship with God. Each person must understand, decide, and surrender his life to God. A person cannot be a Christian by living in a nation that calls itself Christian.

The remnant was made up of a minority of Jews who gained right relationship with God through personal faith.

What about the other Jews who did not believe? 11:7-10

The majority rested in the fact that they were the chosen people They were religious but insensitive to the truth. They were so secure, so self-satisfied, that they went to sleep spiritually. In verse 7 Paul says, *They have been hardened...* The Greek verb used here is "poroun." The noun "porosis" gives a clearer meaning. It is a medical word which means "a callus." It was a word used for the callus which forms around the fracture when a bone is broken. This is the hard bone formation which helps to mend the break. Paul was saying that a callus had grown over the hearts of the people. When a callus grows on any part of the body, that part loses its feeling; it becomes insensitive. This was the spiritual picture of the majority of the Jews.

God used the unbelieving, callused, insensitive Jews to help others.

Salvation of the Gentiles 11:11-24

Through Israel's rejection, a way was opened for salvation to be brought to the non-Jewish world. We must understand this to be part of God's original promise to Abraham. God said, *And through you I will bless all the nations.* Genesis 12:3b In verses 11-16 Paul says that if Israel's failure resulted in blessings and riches for the Gentiles, how much more will Israel's inclusion in grace mean to the whole world. If their partial exclusion has brought such blessings to the world, how much more will the world be blessed when they are included.

In verse 16 Paul speaks of Israel when he talks of the piece of bread and the roots. These are used to illustrate that the Jews can never be totally and finally rejected.

In the Old Testament there was a law (Numbers 15:19-20) that stated if dough was being prepared, the first part was offered to God. When this was done, the whole lump of dough became sacred. The offering of the first part made all of it sacred. Also, when a tree was planted, it was dedicated to God; therefore, every branch that came from it was sacred. There was no need of further dedication as new branches developed.

Paul teaches from this illustration that the very beginning of the Jewish nation was dedicated to God; therefore, the developed nation also must have a special meaning to God. The small tree or the first piece of dough, referred to the great early leaders such as Abraham.

In verses 17-24 Paul uses a long allegory to remind the Gentiles of their privilege and responsibility.

The prophets had often pictured the nation of Israel as the olive tree of God. The olive tree was the most common and useful tree for the Jews. The cultivated olive tree (11:17) represented the Jews. This was the tree planted in gardens and well cared for. The wild olive tree represented the Gentiles. This tree grew in the desert areas, unprotected and uncared for.

It was an undeserved privilege for the wild olive (Gentiles) to be grafted into the family tree of God. Paul warned the Gentiles not to take lightly their privileges and responsibilities. The Gentiles had no reason to boast because the Jews were the natural branches and the Gentiles were only grafted branches. The only reason the Gentiles enjoyed such a privileged relationship with God was because of faith. 11:20

Paul issues a warning in verses 21-22. Every Christian is a Christian because of faith in Christ. No Christian can boast of deserving or earning that relationship to God.

Judaism is the root from which Christianity has sprung. The attitude of the Christian should be gratitude and love for the Jew.

The Hope of Israel 11:25-32

In this passage we see the final outcome of God's redemptive purpose in history and especially the victory for the Jews.
Paul emphasized that the stubborn unbelief of the Jews is temporary. It will last until the Gospel is made known to the Gentiles and God's purpose in the Gentiles' salvation is completed. (11:25)

And this is how all Israel will be saved. (11:26a) The conversion of the Gentiles will stir up the Jews to a realization of their opportunity.

This does not mean that every Jew will be saved. It does mean that every true Jew will be saved. A true Jew is one who has accepted God's way of salvation through faith. It does not include every Jew who was born a Jew, but every Jew born again by faith. There will be a time when many Jews will turn to God, a time when they will cease their efforts to earn salvation through keeping the Law and will turn to God in faith.

Another great truth to observe in this passage is that everything, salvation of both Jews and Gentiles, depends on the mercy of God. There is nothing for man to boast of; all is of God.

This makes us totally dependent on God, which should produce a people of humility and gratitude.

A Song of Praise 11:33-36

This doxology is a testimony to the almightiness of God, the trustworthiness of God, the faithfulness of God.

Paul is saying that God is God and no man can understand Him, know His mind, advise Him, or explain His decisions. All this relates to the sovereignty of God, His mercy, and the free will of man.

There are many things about God and His creation far beyond man's comprehension. We must trust Him to be God of it all. We can sit in awe, trust Him, and praise Him.

Application and Participation

1. Way of salvation ___
   Sovereignty of God ___
   (Place chapter 9 or chapter 10 in the appropriate blanks.)

2. Chapter 11 continues with the Jews' relationship to God.
   True ___ False ___

3. Paul gives two illustrations in the first seven verses to prove that God did not reject His people. Give one of the illustrations.

4. The remnant refers to the majority of the Jews who did not believe. True ____ False ____

5. The unbelief of the Jews opened the way for the _____ to be saved.

6. The word Gentile refers to all people who are not Jews. True ____ False ____

7. Paul had a special ministry to the Gentiles, even though he was a Jew. True ____ False ____

8. The cultivated, garden olive tree, referred to the _____. The wild olive tree referred to the _____.

9. The unbelief of the Jews is temporary, meaning many will be saved in the future. True ____ False ____

10. God is God. What does this mean in light of verses 33-36?

Key verses to memorize: Romans 11:33,36

ROMANS 12

New Relationships

Outline

1. Appeal for Devotion 12:1-2

2. The Christian's Relationship to Other Members of the
   Christian Family 12:3-13

   a. Humility 12:3
   b. Faithful Use of Individual Gifts 12:4-8
   c. Interdependent Union 12:4-8
   d. The Life of Love 12:9-13

3. The Christian's Relationship to the World 12:14-21

The first eleven chapters of Romans are **doctrinal**. The last
chapters are **practical**. Chapters 1-11 deal with how a Christian
is to think. Chapters 12-15:13 deal with how a Christian is to
act.

Paul taught that salvation comes through faith in Christ, as is
taught repeatedly in chapters 1-11. He also taught that genuine
faith produces works—a new kind of life, as we see in chapters
12-15:23.

The theme of the first eleven chapters deals with how God makes a person righteous. Now in chapter 12 Paul states that this righteousness must be demonstrated in righteous living.

In chapters 1-11 God is magnified as the answer for man's (both Jews' and Gentiles') sin problems. It is God who chooses man—saves, forgives, and makes new all who trust in His Son. To be saved from his sinful nature, man must have a God of grace and mercy. This is the picture of chapters 1-11. The climax is seen in 11:33-36.

Romans 12:1-2 is basic and very important. "Therefore," or "so then," point back to all the great truths of chapter 1-11. Because of the grace, mercy, and love of God experienced in the heart of the believer, there is only one reasonable thing to do. This is found in verses 1-2.

Appeal for Devotion 12:1-2

Because Paul knew by experience the teachings of chapters 1-11 to be true, he appealed for devotion and commitment in the lives of believers. (12:1-2)

Some have called verses 1-2 a statement of Christian morality. Others have called it the basis for Christian ethics.

Paul is appealing that the principles and values of Christ be allowed to infiltrate the core (mind) of a person in such a way that the person acts upon these principles. On another occasion Paul said in essence, "Let the mind of Christ be in you." (Philippians 2:5) There is a changing, a renewing of the mind that is necessary before there can be a change of conduct.

We need enough of God within us that we will act as He would act in situations.

There should burst upon us such a climactic insight of who Christ is and what He has done that we must say, "I will give my life to actualize it. It is of such value that I will give my body to be a medium through which, in my actions, I will actualize what God is like." This is true worship.

True worship then becomes more than a song and sermon. For the person who understands and accepts verses 1-2, the universe becomes God's house of worship. The sacrifice offered is a life being lived and completely dedicated to the purposes and glory of God. This life expresses itself through the body of the believer. Therefore, in light of God's goodness to us, each believer must offer his own body to be used by God. This committed body becomes the channel through which the world knows of the love of God.

This is not the kind of religion you can control; it is the kind of religion that controls you. You become the clay under the control of the potter's hands.

Paul is saying, as a result of chapters 1-11, I call on you to take the only way that your mind will conclude to be reasonable.

...*let God transform you inwardly...* (12:2) To change external habits without an inward change is hypocrisy. Only God can change the innermost being of a person.

If society is to be changed, there must be a radical change in the individual minds.

It is a fact that what I do indicates what I believe. What I believe is, therefore, very important. To believe like a Christian will mean that a person will act like a Christian. People will raise their conduct to the level of their inner values. It should be remembered that what we say does not necessarily indicate what we believe.

In these first two verses Paul is saying: This thing that God has done in Christ is so beautiful, so right, that I cannot but give my body as a medium to actualize these values.

As Christians, we are called to live as men and women of a new life. We are no longer to be slaves of the popular habits of humanity. We do not live according to what everyone else is doing.

The Christian's Relationship to Members of the Christian Family 12:3-13

Before going into details of the way a Christian conducts himself among other Christians, Paul reminds the people that he is writing with a God-given authority which comes from the grace of God given to him.

♦ Before actions there should be humility. 12:3

Conceit, vain glory, ego-centeredness, is the chief sin of all man-kind and poses a threat even to the Christian. We are to judge ourselves according to the amount of faith received from God. This leaves no place for pride or boasting. It is important that we honestly assess our own capabilities without conceit and without false modesty. An important ingredient in the fellowship among the family of God is the **examination of real self**.

Each person should realize that he has something to contribute, but no one should have too much of an egotistical picture of himself.

♦ It is important that each member of the Christian family be faithful in using his individual gifts. 12:4-8

Talents are entrusted to us by God, not to use in competition, but in sharing with the talents of others in order to lift all who are related. In God's great family, every member is assigned a special position. The assignment comes from God, not from man. Paul uses this kind of logic in 1 Corinthians 12:12-31.

Though there is oneness in Christ, there are differences. Each person has gifts different from those of others. The difference is caused by the differing grace given us by God. (12:6) Gifts are not to be used for self-glory. God gives us gifts to be used in serving others.

All gifts must be used with a sense of responsibility. A person with one talent does not look down on a person with another talent which may appear less in the public spotlight. A distinction of value should not be made between the singer and the usher, the preacher and the teacher. The present day gap between the "clergy" and the "laity" is not Biblical and is demonic in nature and result.

Every person is extremely important to the welfare of the family because every person has been given a specific gift to contribute to the development of the family of Christ. In verses 6-8 Paul gives a list of seven gifts. This is not an exhaustive list, although most specific gifts may fall under one of these seven general gifts.

You can know your gift if you are searching for God's will in your life.

• Interdependence is beautiful and important in the relationship of God's people. 12:4-8

Each person has good characteristics to share. When many are related, everyone gets the benefit. When good, positive forces unite, there is a unification of strengths. You put in a nickel and you take out a dollar.

When a person puts his talent in the "pot" he takes out much more than he has put in. Look at all the things that come to us by our being a member of society. It is the interdependence of society that makes modern transportation, education, health care, etc., available to all of us.

What are some of the benefits that come to us because we are part of the Christian family? There is love and acceptance, fellowship, encouragement, generosity, leadership, prayer support, etc. Without the union of many members of one family, these blessings would not be ours. It is sad to think that one who has not accepted Christ cannot experience these blessings in their fullness.

There is variety among the members, but there is union with each other because of faith in Christ.

• Among the members of the Christian family, love is a way of life. 12:9-13

Life is an adventure of love for the Christian. There is a special love between believers that is foreign to the unbeliever. Genuine love is based upon this fact: The God-kind of love is that which makes life.

The Greek word for love in verse 9 is "agape." It hardly existed in usage before the time of Christ. Its distinctive meaning must be understood from Christian literature. It is the love of God that can be experienced only by those who know God personally.

In verse 9 Paul says let love be completely sincere. This means without hypocrisy. In Greek drama, "hypocrisy" meant to play a role, or pretend. Paul was saying Christian love has no place for play acting.

Genuine love will have certain characteristics as found in verses 9-13.

1. Opposes evil
2. Acknowledges relationship of brotherhood of believers
3. Is concerned for welfare of others
4. Puts Christ first
5. Is zealous
6. Knows hope, joy, and patience
7. Prizes communion with God
8. Expresses generous hospitality

The Christian's Relationship to the World
12:14-21

The Christian must love the non-Christian.

Romans 12:14-21 gives a list of opportunities for the Christian to show love to the non-Christian.

1. We are to forgive wrongs and insults.
2. We are to share the joys and sorrows of others.
3. We must guard against selfish ambition and pride.
4. We must never pay back evil.
5. We must do the honorable thing.
6. We must strive to be at peace with others.
7. We must leave vengeance to God.
8. We must overcome evil with good.

The Christian has a personal responsibility to live a certain kind of life because God has ordered it. Obedience in Christian conduct comes, not from fear, but because of God's great love and mercy shown to us through His Son. Because He loves us so much and blesses us so much, our only reasonable conclusion is to offer our bodies as a daily living medium to channel His love to the world.

Application and Participation

1. Practical _____   chapters 9-11
   doctrinal _____   chapter 4
   Abraham _____   chapters 1-11
   Sovereignty of God _____   chapters 12-15:13
   Jews _____   chapter 9
   (Write correct chapter or chapters in blanks.)

2. Because of God's mercy and grace, the believer is to offer his body as a living sacrifice. True ____ False ____

3. Paul pictures the church as a body with many parts. True ____ False ____

4. Paul lists seven different gifts. Name as many as you can.

5. The amount of education you have, determines what your gift is. True ____ False ____

6. The Christian is to love only those who are kind. True ____ False ____

7. If someone wrongs you, what should be your response?

8. According to Romans 12, what is true worship?

9. Name some duties of the Christian.

10. Why should the Christian be humble?

Key verses to memorize: Romans 12:1-2

ROMANS 13

Righteousness Demonstrated

Outline

1. The Christian Life Expressed in Citizenship 13:1-7

   a. Respect for Government Authorities 13:1-5
   b. Responsibility to Support Government 13:6-7

2. The Debt of Love 13:8-10

3. Living as People of the Light 13:11-14

The Christian Life Expressed in Citizenship
13:1-7

The Christian has responsibilities not only within the church, to fellow believers, and to individuals outside the faith, but also to the government.

Jesus recognized the government and its helpful work of maintaining order and collecting taxes. (Matthew 17:24-25; 22:15-22; Mark 12:17)

For a clearer understanding of Romans 13:1-7, it is helpful to note that while Jesus recognized the value of government as an institution ordained by God, He criticized the abuses of the government. Jesus called Herod a "fox" (Luke 13:32) and spoke of the leaven of Herod. (Mark 8:15) Jesus condemned power for power's sake, making it clear that the authority of the ruler comes from God. (Mark 10:42-43; John 19:11)

Jesus taught separation of church and state. The two institutions should work as two separate bodies, with unity but not union.

Paul recognized the government as a God-given institution, working to protect the good and to restrain evildoers. The government was to act as God's servant and the instrument of God's wrath against evildoers. Since the government is God's instrument to promote peace and order, it is the duty of all to support it by acting as good citizens, paying taxes, and respecting those in power.

The fact that Paul believed government to be ordained of God does not mean he believed the Christian was to give uncritical obedience to any form of government.

The Christian must live his life as a part of society. He is a citizen of the state. This means he has a Christian responsibility to be a good citizen.

There is one God and the Christian is to worship Him alone. Above all other citizenships, the Christian is a citizen of the Kingdom of God.

The Debt of Love 13:8-10

*Be under obligation to no one...*13:8 Debts can become burdens which affect relationships. A debtor often tries to escape the presence of his creditor. The only way to get rid of existing debts is to pay them. A Christian should never deny or run away from debts.

The main point of this passage deals with the debt no Christian can avoid having and can never repay. This is the debt of love to one another.

The obligation to love is a debt Christians owe to all people. True Christian love is not selective; it includes all. The love of God exercised by the Christian sees the worth and dignity of every person, no matter what or who he may be.

Paul says whoever loves his fellowman has obeyed the Law. (13:8) The apostle quotes five of the Ten Commandments, the five most fundamental in human relations. A person who loves will not commit adultery, or steal, or kill, or bear false witness, or covet. We are reminded of the summary of the Law expressed by Jesus in the two great commandments as recorded in Mark 12:30-31. *"...Love the Lord your God with all your heart, with all your soul, with all your mind, and with all your strength." The second most important commandment is this: "Love your neighbor as you love yourself." There is no other commandment more important than these two.*

The whole Law is summed up in one word: love. Love at its minimum will never do your neighbor any harm. Love at its maximum liberates, sets free, lifts, helps the other to become what God has intended him to be.

Living as People of the Light 13:11-14

Paul said Christians are to live as children of the light. He expected Jesus to return at any time, therefore, he urged the people to be alert, to live in the light, to walk as people of the light. If the message was true in Paul's day, then it certainly is true today. The signs have been fulfilled and Jesus could come back at any moment.

Christians who expect Jesus to return at any time will love and live differently than those who do not expect Him to come soon. The King is coming and few are preparing. When an important person, such as the president of a nation, passes a certain route, there is much preparation and excitement. The King of Kings is coming; are we preparing?

Paul lists six sins that characterize life without Christ. (13:13)

1. Orgies - The Greek word is "komos." This meant a noisy band of revelers who roamed the city streets at night. They became a nuisance, disturbing others.

2. Drunkenness - For the well being of others a Christian will abstain from intoxicating beverages of all kinds. Beer, wine, and all alcoholic drinks, bring destruction to individuals and society. A Christian shows an insensitivity to the welfare of others when he sells or consumes alcoholic drinks.

3. Immorality - This may take many forms. It is primarily concerned with fidelity in marriage, adultery, and perversion of sex. The pagan world is marked by sexual perversion as we have read in Romans 1.

4. Indecency - This describes the person who knows no shame. He does not care who sees him in his sin. He feels no need to keep his sins secret. He has fallen so deep into sin that he is no longer ashamed of anything he does.

5. Fighting - This is a spirit that comes from an uncontrolled and unholy competition. It comes from the strong desire for place, power, and prestige. This characterizes the person who cannot take second place. Self must be exalted above all else.

6. Jealousy - This speaks of the person who cannot be content with what he has. He looks with a jealous eye on every blessing given to someone else and denied to himself.

In conclusion Paul urges the believers in Rome to stop giving attention to things that destroy and to give attention to the things of Christ. This requires taking up the weapons of Christ. The greatest weapon of all is love. By living a life of love, evil can be overcome.

Application and Participation

1. Romans 13 deals with the Christian's relation to

   _____.

2. Paul believed that government was ordained by God.
   True ____ False ____

3. Because the Christian is a member of the Kingdom of God, he has no responsibility to any earthly government.
   True ____ False ____

4. The Christian should respect government leaders.
   True ____ False ____

5. The way of supporting the government is given in Romans 13. It is by paying _____.

6. A Christian has the responsibility of paying his debts.
   True ___ False ___

7. There is a debt which the Christian owes to every person. It is _____.

8. Paul lists five of the Ten Commandments, saying the law of love fulfills all five of them. Name three of the commandments.

9. *The night is nearly over, day is almost here.* What was Paul speaking of when he said that?

10. Paul says Christians, as children of light, are to live a certain kind of life. He names six sins which should not be in the Christian's life. Name two of these sins.

11. If there is a conflict between the teachings of the government and the teachings of God, which is to be followed and why?

Key verse to memorize: Romans 13:8

ROMANS 14

Constructive Influences

Outline

1. Concern for Weak Brothers 14:1-12

    a. The weak are to be accepted. 14:1
    b. Believers, strong or weak, are not to judge others. 14:3-4
    c. Personal convictions are to be developed and held in
       relationship to God. 14:5-12
       1) God is to receive glory. 14:6-8
       2) Every person must answer to Christ. 14:10-12

2. The Importance of Influence 14:13-23

    a. Do not use Christian freedom to cause others to fall.
       14:13-16
    b. The Christian is to seek the Kingdom of God first.
       14:17-20
    c. The Christian is to practice self-denial if it will help the
       brothers. 14:21-23

Paul continues to describe the kind of life that is acceptable and pleasing to God, which in the light of God's mercy and grace, is the only reasonable way we can live. (Romans 12:1-2) Because of the privilege of knowing Christ personally, every Christian has a responsibility to live like a Christian in his relationship to other people.

In chapter 14 Paul deals with a very practical problem which every church experiences.

Concern for Weak Christians 14:1-12

Paul was concerned about how those strong in the faith treated the ones who were weak.

We need to recognize that there will be differences among church members. It is helpful to remember that it is not bad to disagree—as long as we can disagree agreeably. When love is strong, differences and disagreements will not divide or destroy the church.

There are various kinds of differences. There are doctrinal differences. There are different ways to worship, some formal and some informal. In this chapter the problem concerned matters of individual consciences. These are matters that have no direct commandments from God to give direction.

The two major illustrations given in this chapter are the matters of eating and special days. One believed it was allowable to eat anything; another who was weak ate only vegetables.

It is helpful to understand the background of these people. They were Jewish people who had been slaves to the many exaggerated laws of the Scribes and Pharisees. There were many sects and religions in the ancient world which observed very strict food laws. The Jews had their laws concerning food, as seen in Leviticus. Some new converts to Christianity were weak in the faith and continued to cling to parts of the Jewish law to which they had been slaves. Paul describes the strong in the faith as those who were free from slavery to the Law. God has never intended that any person be a slave to the Law or that the Law be the master of a person. This has never been the purpose of the Law, but the Jewish religion had become a matter of keeping rules. It had become a slavery rather than a relationship.

Paul had some definite words of advice for these two groups to help them live and prosper together in the same church.

The weak brothers are to be accepted. 14:1

The strong are not to argue with the weak about things that are a matter of personal conscience. This does not mean a church is to accept a person as a member even if his life is wicked. If a person does not eat meat because he feels it is unhealthy, that is his opinion and should be respected. On the other hand, if a person does not believe the Bible to be God's Word, he should not be accepted as a member. While it is his opinion, it contradicts the clear teachings of the Bible. Make an issue only of those things which are issues. Do not fight over something that is not really a problem.

People do not qualify to judge others. 14:3-4

Paul says no person has a right to criticize another person's servant. The servant is responsible to his master alone. Every believer is a servant of God. Only God has the right to judge each servant. A person does not stand or fall because of our judgment, but because of God's judgment. No person is qualified to criticize or condemn another. We must try to understand and love each other and leave the judging to God.

Personal convictions are to be developed and held in relationship to God. 14:5-12

Each person must study his relationship to God and personally decide what is best for himself. Honor and glory given to God should be a major determining factor in the convictions and opinions held by each person. No believer should do anything for his own honor and glory, whether it is eating meat or not eating meat. Whether the believer is considered weak or strong, the thing that counts is the motive—is it to bring honor and attention to self or to God?

Every person will stand before God to give an account of the way he lived on earth. The weak are not to be judged by the strong. The strong are not to be judged by the weak. All, both weak and strong, will stand before God, the Righteous Judge.

The Importance of Influence 14:13-23

Influence is important. Some are caused to stand while others are caused to fall because of influence of fellow believers.

The strong Christian is not to use his freedom to cause a weaker Christian to stumble. 14:13-16

It is sin to cause another to stumble in the faith. Read Matthew 18:6. Paul said the question is not to be decided on the basis that meat is clean or not clean. The unclean meat spoken of here was meat that had been offered to idols. In the eyes of the new, weaker believer, it was wrong to eat this meat. The stronger believer did not see anything wrong with eating it. Paul advised the strong believer: *Do not let the food that you eat ruin the man for whom Christ died!* 14:15b

101

This means every habit must be analyzed to see if it is causing a brother to stumble. There may be something which in itself is not wrong, but if it causes a brother to stumble, it becomes wrong to do it.

It is the duty of every believer to think of everything not as it affects ourselves only, but also as it affects others. We have no right to cause another person to stumble by doing things that are not really important. A Christian cannot escape responsibility for his influence.

The Kingdom of God must have first place in the life of the believer. 14:17-20

There are more important things than keeping special days or eating meat. The Kingdom is not a matter of rules and regulations established by man. The Kingdom is not something external or ceremonial.

In 14:17-20 Paul is dealing with the problem of the strong in the faith abusing or taking advantage of his new-found freedom. When a Jew became a Christian, he found that all the insignificant rules and regulations were done away with. The danger was that he might interpret Christianity as a new-found freedom to do as he pleased.

We must remember that Christian freedom and Christian love must never be separated. Paul is reminding the believers that the Kingdom of God does not consist of eating and drinking what one likes.

The Kingdom of God consists of three great things, **righteousness**, **peace**, and **joy** (14:17), all of which are others-centered. If a person strives for these three things, there will not be time to give attention to little things that do not matter. When a church forgets its true purpose and begins giving time to unimportant things, a sickness invades the fellowship. The pursuit of differences of opinion tears down. The pursuit of righteousness, peace, and joy builds up the church.

Righteousness - This is a matter of right relationships to God and to man. When God's love is in our hearts, the welfare and feelings of the other person become more important than our own. Others first, self last.

Peace - The Christian has a new freedom, a freedom to live at peace with his fellowman. He is free to sacrifice so that peace may reign. God is in the business of bringing peace to man, and this becomes the business of every believer.

Joy - This does not mean trying to make ourselves happy; it means making others happy. Joy comes to the Christian when he brings joy to others, even if it means not doing some things such as eating meat offered to idols.

In verse 18 we see that anyone giving priority to righteousness, peace, and joy must become a slave to Jesus. This means the Christian has complete freedom—to do what Christ likes.

The Christian has a responsibility to pursue those things which help build up the church. No one is to use his Christian freedom in a way that will destroy others. (14:19-20)

The believer is to practice self-denial if it will help others.
14:21-23

103

Paul gives a general rule which applies to every action or habit. *The right thing to do is to keep from eating meat, drinking wine, or doing anything else that will make your brother fall.* 14:21

The use of alcoholic beverages can never be justified because it destroys the body and has a bad influence on others. A man may say, "I can drink a few beers and it will not hurt me." (Only a person uninformed about the effects of beer will say such a thing.) Perhaps he is able to drink moderately and not become an alcoholic. But if he has children who take up their father's habits, he has encouraged them by his example. It is probable that the use of alcohol will have devastating effects on at least one of the children. The father bears the responsibility of his influence. The same can be said of habits of smoking, gluttony, worldly entertainment, etc.

If a person is free in Christ, he will be able to enjoy the freedom to say no to some things. A person who cannot say no is not free, but is a slave to self and things. A true Christian can deny himself many things for the sake of others.

In 14:22 Paul tells the stronger Christian not to make big news of his freedom to eat meat, etc. This kind of boasting may cause hurt to the immature believer.

All the Christian does should be based on faith—faith in God—a faith relationship that will give light on what is right and wrong in daily life. Paul gives a final word of advice in verse 23: "If there is a doubt, don't do it."

Application and Participation

1. In Romans 14 Paul talked about the strong Christian and the _____ Christian.

2. The strong in the faith are to accept the weaker brother.
True ___ False ___

3. Why did the weaker brothers think eating meat was wrong?

4. Was Paul against observing the Lord's Day?

5. The strong in the faith are qualified to judge the weak.
True ___ False ___

6. Every person must stand before Christ and give account of the life he has lived. True ___ False ___

7. If a weak brother stumbles because of what I do, it is his fault because he is weak. True ___ False ___

8. The Kingdom of God is more than eating meat; it consists of three things. Name them.

9. How are these three things unselfish?

10. When does right become wrong?

Key verse to memorize: Romans 14:19

ROMANS 15

Traits Of Righteousness

Outline

1. Marks of True Discipleship 15:1-13

    a. Others-centered 15:1-4
        1) Help Weak Carry Burdens 15:1
        2) Put Others First 15:2
        3) The Example of Christ 15:3
        4) The Voice of the Scripture 15:4

    b. Unity 15:5-13
        1) God the Source 15:5
        2) Christ the Example 15:5
        3) Praise the Purpose 15:6
        4) Illustrated by All-inclusiveness of Jews and Gentiles
           15:7-13

2. Marks of a Righteous Person 15:14-33

    a. Confidence in Others 15:14
    b. Recognition of Position as a Servant 15:16
    c. Acceptance of Privilege and Responsibility of Priesthood
       15:16
    d. Glory in Being a Chosen Instrument 15:17-19
    e. A Person of Vision Who Pioneers the Frontiers 15:20-29
    f. A Person of Courage Bathed in Prayer 15:30-33

The theme of Romans is: How God Makes a Person Righteous. Chapters 1-11 contain the strong doctrinal teaching of how God in His sovereignty is at work dealing with the sinner to transform him into a saint. Chapters 12-15 are practical, portraying the kind of life lived by the righteous person.

Chapter 15 gives a great summary statement of the marks of true righteousness and the marks of a righteous person.

Marks of True Discipleship 15:1-13

1. Others-centeredness 15:1-4

Sin is self-centeredness. To be made righteous means to be made the opposite, others-centered. Confusion, turmoil, and fighting result when people think more about their own welfare than the welfare of others. A righteous person does not always have to get his way in order to be happy.

• If we are others-centered, we will help the weak to carry their burdens. (15:1)

It should be pointed out that this verse does not say the strong are to carry the burdens of the weak. A major principle of healthy human development is seen here. If the strong desire to destroy the weak, they should carry the burdens of the weak. If the strong desire to help the weak, they must **help** the weak to carry their burdens. There is a major difference between carrying the burdens of the weak and helping the weak carry their own burdens. This difference is seen in verse 2.

• The purpose and result of helping the weak to carry his burden is **to build him up in the faith.** (15:2)

The ministry of the strong should be designed to help the weak to become strong—not to relieve him of responsibility. Let's say, for example, that a church is going to build a new meeting place. There is a friend of the church who is interested in the building project. This friend has much more money than the economically weak church members. The construction of the building is a burden calling for great sacrifice. Because of not having a strong independent, self-sufficient background, the natural thing for the members is to hope for a building through the generosity of the rich friend. Out of a perverted love, the rich friend may yield and carry the burden of the weak. What is the result? It gives more power and prestige to the rich friend and relieves the weak members of a needed responsibility. The members remain weak because they have been robbed of the growing experience of learning to carry their own burdens. They have depended on someone else to carry the burdens for them. A pattern is formed.

What happens after the rich friend pays for the building? Such a building needs nice furnishings. Who will pay for them?

The strong person has a responsibility to **help** the weak person carry his burden. A constructive principle in human relationships always worth following is: Help people to help themselves. This is a helping that builds people up in the faith.

• Christ serves as our example in being others-centered. 15:3

Paul says in Philippians 2:3-7, *Don't do anything from selfish ambition, or from a cheap desire to boast; but be humble toward each other, never thinking you are better than others. And look out for each other's interests, not just for your own. The attitude you should have is the one that Christ Jesus had: He always had the very nature of God, but he did not think that by force he should try to become equal with God. Instead, of his own free will he gave up all, and he took the nature of a servant.*

Christ gave Himself for others because His interest centered in others. He is our example to turn from our self-centered way of life to begin living for others.

♦ The Scripture encourages us to be others-centered. (15:4)

From the beginning of the Old Testament to the conclusion of the New Testament, the story of God's redemption shows God to be others-centered.

The others-centered person is filled with hope because life is bigger than himself; it includes others. We need the Word of God to supply us with patience and encouragement in our relationship with others.

2. Unity 15:5-13

♦ God is the source of unity. 15:5

God is the "enabler." He will ...*enable you to have the same point of view among yourselves.* Premiers and Presidents sit at peace conferences searching for unity among nations but forget to acknowledge the Prince of Peace.

Christians must depend on God to give unity. Man can submit to God in faith and find unity among the brothers.

We see unity in the nature of God. He is one. He is not contradictory in his nature. He does not lie or deceive—He is true.

The work of God reveals unity. All creation is a masterpiece of unity—from the changing seasons to the germination of a seed.

* Christ is an example of unity. 15:5

In John 12:44-45, Jesus said, *Whoever believes in me believes not only in me but also in him who sent me. Whoever sees me sees also him who sent me.* This is only one of several times that Jesus claimed unity with the Father.

Christ had singleness of purpose. His purpose was in harmony with His Father's purpose.

Three phrases found in verses 5 and 6 indicate unity as a mark of true righteousness. They are: "same point of view," "together," and "one voice."

* The purpose of unity is praise to God. 15:6

Through the enabling power of God, believers can be unified, having the same point of view, so that with one voice God will be praised.

Often disunity and hard feelings come because people are seeking praise. There is no limit to what could be accomplished if we did not mind who gets the praise. Sometimes someone will say, "I did all that and nobody paid me any attention." Who should be praised because of the work of a believer? If the believer is doing it for God, then God deserves the praise. Two preachers preach a sermon. After hearing one, the crowd goes away saying, "How great a preacher he is." After hearing the other preacher, the crowd goes away saying, "What a great Savior we have." Who has preached the better sermon?

True unity brings praise to the Father because true unity is possible only because of and through the Father.

♦ The inclusion of the Jews and Gentiles in God's plan illustrates unity. 15:7-13

This is Paul's final plea for all to be accepted on the basis of faith in God. In God's plan all are important. Everybody is somebody. All fit together to make a unified whole. The weak must be a part of the whole, otherwise there would not be the strong. All make one body. There is a single fellowship in the family of God. There may be many differences but only one Christ. The bond of unity is a common loyalty to Him.

As we see in 15:7-13, Christ was Christ of the Jew and also of the Gentile. He was born a Jew, but He ministered to both Jew and Gentile. Christ is an all inclusive Savior. His followers must know a unity which is made up of every part of the body of Christ. In the church each must be accepted as a necessary part of the whole.

Unity is a distinguishing mark of true righteousness—unity with God, self, and fellow believers.

Marks of a Righteous Person 15:14-33

1. The righteous person will have confidence in others. 15:14

Many times people will not do any more than they are expected to do. A child will do much more in life if the parents believe he is able. A young preacher will preach better if someone thinks he can. Confidence is contagious.

Paul had confidence in the Christians at Rome. He said, *I myself feel sure that you are full of goodness, that you have all knowledge, and that you are able to teach one another.* 15:14

Paul did not look down on people. He saw them eye to eye as brothers. He did not assume to have final and superior knowledge and goodness. He spoke of their goodness and knowledge.

Perhaps the Romans had not been to school in Jerusalem, but they were able to teach one another. We have little Biblical basis for the hierarchy present in some churches where there is one pastor or teacher who is the only one acknowledged as capable to lead and teach. It is a tradition that has almost become a Protestant papacy. The Christians at Rome were able to teach each other. This meant more than one teacher and more than a few "elected" teachers.

Paul believed in the ability of people surrendered to Christ.

2. The righteous person will understand servanthood. 15:16

The title Paul most often used to describe himself was "slave" or "servant." This was not a false, shallow humility. Paul was nobody, was nothing as far as he was concerned, except in relation to Christ.

The kind of servanthood we see in Paul produced boldness. Often we have the negative idea that servanthood is characterized by weakness, timidity, and fearfulness. This may be the result of being a servant to another man, but it is different to serve God. To be a slave to Christ brings freedom, peace, joy, boldness, and security.

112

Servanthood and its fruits can be known only when Christ becomes the Master and all the slave does in life is related to Christ. Only a minority in most churches have ever experienced Servanthood. It is meant to be for every believer.

3. A righteous person will experience the *privilege* and *responsibility* of being a priest. 15:16

Paul said, "I serve as a priest." A brief study of Paul's life will reveal that his idea of a priest is not the same as the ideas that have come from Rome. According to the Bible, every believer is called to be a priest. A priest is one who has received salvation through faith in Christ and feels a strong daily responsibility to share the Good News with others. He does this in words and actions. Priesthood is for the farmer, the businessman, the poor, the rich, the educated, the uneducated. The privilege and responsibility is the same for all.

4. Being a channel and instrument is position enough for the righteous. 15:17-19

Paul said it was only his union with Christ that was worth talking about. What God does through that union is what counts. *I will be bold and speak only of what Christ has done through me to lead the Gentiles to obey God.* (15:18a) All believers need to be more like this, filled less with "I did's" and more with "Christ did's." Paul magnified Christ, not himself. A Christian is to be an instrument to be used by God alone.

5. A righteous person pioneers a new frontier because he has a vision. 15:20-29

This is clearly evident in Paul's life. *My ambition has always been to proclaim the Good News in places where Christ has not*

113

been heard of... (15:20a) Paul longed to go to Spain (15:28) which was the limit of the civilized world as he knew it. That was as far as he could go with the Gospel. Spain stood out in Paul's mind also because it was the frontier of the arts and intellects. Many of the great thinkers came from there. Paul wanted to introduce the Gospel to such people so they could influence the world for Christ.

A righteous person is never satisfied while there are frontiers to be pioneered for Christ. A pioneer is one who is deeply motivated to initiate the exploration of the unknown. The love of God motivates, the Holy Spirit leads in initiation. People without Christ are the known "unknown."

What about a near-by neighborhood or town with no Gospel-preaching church? We need righteous people with a vision to reach out.

6. Courage bathed in prayer is a mark of a righteous person.
15:30-33

As far as we know, Paul never went to Spain. He went on to Jerusalem where he was arrested. He then spent four years in prison, two years in Caesarea and two in Rome.

When Paul went to Jerusalem he knew what he was doing. He was aware of the dangers awaiting him, yet he was determined to go. He requested one thing: *Join me in praying fervently to God for me.* (15:30b) These last verses of the chapter talk of dangers faced and the need for prayer. Paul faced these dangers with courage saturated with prayer.

A righteous person is in daily communion with God through prayer. It may be prayers of consultation, meditation, consecration, or praise; but the righteous person prays.

Application and Participation

1. List two marks of true righteousness.

2. How can the strong help the weak to help themselves?

3. If the strong carry all the burdens of the weak, how does it destroy the weak and the strong?

4. If self-centeredness is the basic nature of sin, what is the basic nature of righteousness?

5. Unity is illustrated in Romans 15 as Paul shows that the plan of God is all inclusive. What two groups are included to make unity?

6. A mark of a righteous person is confidence in others. How does confidence in another's abilities help that person? How has someone's confidence in you made a difference in your life?

7. Who may become a priest?

8. A believer is an instrument to be used by God for the welfare of others. True ____ False ____

9. If I am righteous, what hinders me from going to new areas to tell the Good News? Name one town or neighborhood that needs a new church.

Conclusion

Outline

1. Recommendation 16:1-2

2. Personal Greetings 16:3-16

3. Final Instructions 16:17-20

4. Greetings from Others 16:21-24

5. Concluding Prayer of Praise 16:25-27

Recommendation 16:1-2

Paul introduces and recommends Phoebe as a sister in the faith. Phoebe came from Cenchreae, a port of Corinth. She was going to Rome and was going to carry the letter with her.

Personal Greetings 16:3-16

Twenty-four individuals are mentioned by name in this chapter. Six of these are women, which points out Paul's confidence in the place of women in God's work, even in a day when women were not properly recognized.

Of the twenty-four names, thirteen can be found in inscriptions or documents which have to do with the imperial household and Emperor's palace in Rome. This tells us that Christianity had reached into important places of authority.

Briefly notice some of the names.

Priscilla (Prisca in some translations) and Aquila first lived in Rome. They are first mentioned in Acts 18:2. All the Jews were forced to leave Rome in A.D. 52 following an edict by Claudius. From Rome Priscilla and Aquila went to Corinth. They were tent makers, which was Paul's trade, and he lived with them. From Acts 18:18 we learn when Paul left Corinth to go to Ephesus, Priscilla and Aquila went with him.

At Ephesus, Priscilla and Aquila took in the great scholar, Apollos and taught him more about the Christian faith. (Acts 18: 24-26) While at Ephesus, Paul wrote the first letter to the Corinthians. From 1 Corinthians 16:19 we see that Priscilla and Aquila were still at Ephesus. A church met in their house.

After several years the Jews were permitted to go back to Rome. Priscilla and Aquila were among the Jews who returned. Note that a church was again meeting in their house.

What a wonderful testimony. Wherever they went they started a new church which met in their house.

We need Priscillas and Aquilas today to start a church in every unevangelized neighborhood. "But I am only a businessman." So were they. "But I am only a farmer." Theirs was a similar vocation. "But this is my home community and I can't be effective here." They were from Rome and it was there that a church met in their house.

Of all the other names, we know little. A close study will reveal that these were people who were outstanding Christians. Some of them were slaves, palace personnel, men and women with different backgrounds and vocations, but to Paul all were important because they were servants of Jesus Christ.

Today people tend to bow low to individuals with money or world prestige. Not so with Paul. Tent makers headed the list, not because of their work of tent making, but because of a brotherhood that knows no class distinction.

Final Instructions 16:17-20

Paul had a difficult time ending his letter. He warns the Roman believers about people who cause divisions and lead them astray, telling them to stay away from such people. The kind of troublemaker Paul is speaking of, often enjoys debating and philosophizing on subjects that are not important for people to understand. It is a waste of time and often harmful to permit these people to use valuable time to bring confusion. Paul says these people are serving their own appetites. They call attention to themselves by trying to publicly demonstrate their intelligence, which is not intelligence at all.

Don't believe everything that sounds good. It is amazing how easily a person can catch the attention of a new group of believers and lead them almost anywhere. If a person has money and seeming prestige and is a good speaker, it does not necessarily mean that he is really somebody with something to say. Wisdom to know the difference is needed by God's people.

Greetings from Others 16:21-24

Timothy was Paul's "right-hand man," his son in the ministry. Tertius was the secretary who took the dictation from Paul. Gaius was the man in whose house the church met. It appears there was not a mega-church in Rome, but churches scattered where the people lived. It seems there was more than one church in Rome. One met in the house of Priscilla and Aquila and one met in the house of Gaius, and it is probable that others also existed in the city.

Concluding Prayer of Praise 16:25-27

The first part of this prayer says, *Let us give glory to God,* and in the final part Paul says, *To the only God...be the glory.* From beginning to end all is of God, through God, and for God; and all praise is for Him alone.

Application and Participation

1. Who carried the letter to Rome?

2. Did Paul write the letter or did someone else? Who was the secretary?

3. Where did the early Christians worship?

4. Why does God deserve praise?

5. Who would you prefer to get the praise for something you do? God or you?

Final Questions on Romans

1. What is the theme of the Letter to the Romans?

2. Who.is the author of the Letter to the Romans?

3. List five great doctrines found in Romans.

4. There are three "mountain top" passages which we have noted in Romans. What are the chapters?

5. Why is the study of the Letter to the Romans needed in our churches today?

6. How has this study helped you in your Christian development?